MANAGEMENT INFORMATION SYSTEMS
Planning, Developing, Managing

MANAGEMENT INFORMATION SYSTEMS

Planning, Developing, Managing

ARNOLD O. PUTNAM

Pitman

PITMAN PUBLISHING LIMITED
39 Parker Street, London WC2B 5PB

Associated Companies
Copp Clark Pitman, Toronto
Fearon Pitman Publishers Inc, San Francisco
Pitman Publishing New Zealand Ltd, Wellington
Pitman Publishing Pty Ltd, Melbourne

© Arnold O. Putnam 1977

First published in Great Britain 1980
By arrangement with Herman Publishing, Inc., Boston, MA U.S.A.

ISBN   0 273 01450 1

Contents

ACKNOWLEDGMENTS

When a book takes 10 years to develop and finish, the trail of acknowledgments grows very long, but all the more necessary. In treating these by groups for purpose of easy identification, I recognize the difficulty in dealing with the relative support, and hope that those affected understand.

The Cover

This single visual concept has had a great impact upon me and upon my consulting style and further strengthened my support of the blending of the behavioral sciences and management technology. All too frequently the emotional attachments to divisional or functional prestige or preroga-tives have been counter to the intellectual needs of good interfunctional and EDP interface. Progress proceeds at a snail's pace until this is overcome. When intellect shows the managers that they all gain tremendously by helping with the joint MIS development, and an understanding of their emotional problems (usually fears) is achieved—*progress zooms!*

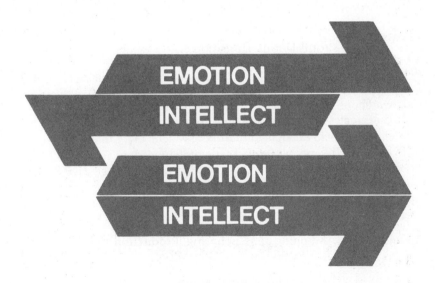

This visual was supplied by *Fred Zweig, President of Waymaker Institute,* St. Louis, Mo., during a consulting assignment at Rath & Strong on our corporate mission.

Colleagues at Rath & Strong

Almost everyone in a small consulting company contributes to its image in some way—but in the preparation of this book I particularly appreciated:

- The editorial review performed by *Robert Cronan*
- The explication of concepts and rewriting of the behavioral sections by *Dan Ciampa*
- The help of *Woodrow Chamberlain* and *Robert Cronan* in preparing the Nordberg Machinery Group MRP case study
- The assistance of the Task Force on the Mapping case study, including *Romeyn Everdell, E. Robert Barlow, Gerald Dorman, William Leitch, Dan Ciampa,* and others.

Many of the above participated with me in a variety of assignments over the 10 years during which the data was collected; others in Rath & Strong include *LeRoy Lindgren, J. Nicholas Edwards, Dan Murray, Wood Sutton, John Noon, Clint Jones,* and *Tom Woods.* I cannot go on without thanking *Sylvia Poster* and *Mim Karhumaa* for much editing and keeping the additions, deletions, and other changes under good control.

Clients' Personnel

The most demanding of the systems installations over the 10 years were those Material Requirements Planning Systems, and Shop Floor and Production Control Systems in complex jobs shops, though some of the multiwarehouse distribution systems, were very demanding.

The greatest contribution came from the installation of MRP and Master Scheduling Controls at Nordberg Machinery Group of Rexnord, Milwaukee.* The people who made it happen are *Robert Schoner,* President, Process Machinery Division; *Eugene Schloesser,* EDP Systems Manager; *Frank Strang,* the General Manager; and *Don Taylor,* President of the Machinery Group. I should also mention *Ron Borowski,* Systems Development, and *Frank Monfre,* Inventory Control Manager, who worked very closely with the Rath & Strong staff previously mentioned.

Probably the smoothest MRP Shop Floor Production Control Program was at the Jones & Lamson Division of Waterbury Farrel—a Textron Company. Three factors contributed to this:

- Jones & Lamson Management, including *Robert Jones,* General Manager, *Ray Streeter,* Factory Manager, *Paul Van Dusen,* Materials

---

* See Case Study Appendix 2.

Control Manager, and *Don Richmond,* a key system analyst and programmer. This group are about as straightforward "let's get on with the job guys" as you could expect.

- Jones & Lamson did not have a lot of other computerized systems with which the MRP and Shop-Floor Control System had to interface.

- Excellent client–consultant relationship based on substantial past history.

The installation most dependent on the contributions of our Organization and Management Dynamics Group (OMD–behavioral scientists) was the distribution system at Leviton. In fact, most of the systems work had been completed, but inaccuracies and user noninvolvement factors prevented its successful use. The Leviton personnel who were instrumental in its success were Don Hendler, Distribution Vice President; Steve Sokolow, EDP Systems Vice President; Tom Blumberg, Marketing Vice President; Harold Leviton, President; Ralph DeBiasi, Financial Vice President; Harvey Kramm, Operations Vice President—Jack Amsterdam, Chairman; and many warehouse managers and task force members.

Another program involving OMD was the Mapping Case Study (See Appendix 1) carried out with Ray Howland, Sr., Chairman, and Roger Howland, President of Eastern Tool and Stamping Co.

At the Hesston Corporation we were involved in a number of successful multidisciplinary (Behavioral Sciences, plus Management Technology) programs, one of which included Data Accuracy and W-I-P Control. Key people were Richard Huxman, Factory Manager; Howard Brenneman, President; Frank Depew, Vice President, Farm Equipment Division (now with Jacobson Manufacturing Co.); Glen Otte, Materials Manager, and many others.

Others include Robert Pash, Vice President, Finance, Newell Companies; Ed Puth, Financial Vice President, and Jim Osborne of EAI; George L.N. Meyer, Jr., then President of the Meyer Group of ATO; Brooke Reeve, President, Harvey Granger, Vice President, Manufacturing, and Vic Johnson, Vice President, Materials, Great Dane Trailers, Inc.; Harreld DeMunbrun, of Casco (now with Echlin), and Stuart Mason, Vice President, Manufacturing; Arthur Williams, formerly EDP Manager of B.F. Goodrich; James Brown, EDP Systems Manager, United Carr Fastener; at Computer Sciences, Infonet Division, Maury Pratt and Marty DeFranco; at Joy Manufacturing Company, Bill Campbell, Distribution Manager, Louis Helmick, President; Larry Greenhouse, Division Manager and Bill Calder, Plant Manager; at Moog, Bill Godin and Bob Brady; and George Raymond, President of Raymond Corporation.

Closer to home, my son, Tim Putnam, did some of the early editing and rearranging that was most helpful, and Dot, my wife, put up with a great deal of "book work"—some even on vacations.

Introduction

This is a book about the successful management of Management Information Systems covering:

- The management requirements, from the Chief Executive to the Systems Programmer.
- The time period from predesign through development, installation, and operation, on to future considerations.

Other books have covered quite thoroughly the technical requirements for Management Information Systems (MIS) in the various functional areas. A few have dealt with some of the key managerial factors for success that are included here. To my knowledge, however, no previous work has tried to compile the managerial factors for successful MIS application as done in this book, i.e., from top-to-bottom of the management and from start-to-finish of the application, based upon more than two dozen case experiences. Yet most professionals correlate the degree of success with MIS more to managerial and human factors than to technical ones.

In the '73 and '74 National APICS Conferences, the author asked several hundred attendees about the biggest cause of poor MIS performance with this response:

	Yes	No
Are you satisfied with the total progress of your MIS system?	20%	80%
Do you consider the most significant determinant to your progress is systems or technical expertise?	20%	80%
Or communications, understanding and human problems?	80%	20%

This test elicited similar responses when asked of several local groups. It remains a mystery as to why this quandary exists: 80% of the problems lie on the human side, yet 95% of the time and money has been spent on further *technical* improvements.

One of the reasons is that the communications and human-resource problems are multifunctional, and the support and planning required have to come from top management. Another reason is the lack of understanding of the type of participation and training required. The routine "lay it on" approach should be replaced by the participative, workshop, "own-my-share-of-the-problem" style. This can best be accomplished with guidance from management development professionals.

The early chapters of the book,

- Getting Started,
- Preparing Top Management for a Key Role in MIS, and
- Creating a Positive Environment for Change,

are directed especially toward top management because this is the crucial stage for its involvement. That which is done or left undone at this stage seriously affects the potential for full success downstream. The latter chapters:

- Designing the System,
- Implementing an MIS System, and
- Living with an MIS System,

are pointed more toward members of middle and lower management, since they have major responsibilities during these stages. The final chapter, "In the Future," has both top management and operating management implications.

Thus, the audience for the book includes:

- Chief executives;
- Functional executives—finance, production, marketing distribution, engineering;
- Departmental managers;
- Production and inventory control managers;
- Materials managers;
- MIS managers;
- EDP managers;
- Systems and programming personnel;
- College students.

The book also deals with the important factor of managing the operation while implementing a Management Information System. Many companies have found the transition period exceedingly difficult and often very costly.

Outline

The first chapter opens with a statement on MIS philosophy. This is followed by a brief historical development of some of the key issues.

The second chapter, "Preparing Top Management for a Key Role in MIS," emphasizes that more is needed than superficial support or acceptance of a program to "keep up with the Joneses." Methods of surveying potential costs and benefits are outlined, together with the commitments that are needed from top management in order to achieve the established goals. The need for a comprehensive master plan and adequate macro designs is outlined. Top management has to provide the active support that overcomes functional barriers and facilitates the achievement of common objectives.

The third chapter, "Creating a Positive Environment for Change," deals with management from top to bottom. Acceptance of change and acceptance of the risk of being wrong must be actively promoted at the top, or progress will be slow and commitment low all the way to the bottom. "Mapping" of Organization Effectiveness and Resource Efficiency is explained in this chapter and a case example is presented in the Appendix.

The human side of MIS and the use of participative training groups to deal with resistance to change is explained. Such methods replace resistance with involvement and goal-setting. At the functional executive level, we need commitment to coordinate with other functions on the program, as well as wholehearted support within each function. In the major "user" departments, such as production and inventory control, sales, distribution, etc., the manager has to play the *full* user role, setting the specifications, checking on progress, clearing up input data, and using the results. Finally, in the EDP and systems area, we need a competent staff that can work effectively with a variety of functional users and encourage their active participation.

The next chapter, "Designing the System," deals with the fundamentals for long-term success rather than with short-term objectives. While the latter may be vital for current support of the application, lack of a long-term view has resulted in perpetual and wasteful rework in many installations. The development of a master plan and macro designing are key steps. The cost of redoing and replacing a badly segmented system can exceed the initial cost, and may create difficult transitional problems as well. Such items as these are explained:

- Integrated data base,
- Management by exception,
- Data edit and check,
- Documentation,
- Modular design,
- Software, including application packages, and
- Systems sensitivity.

The emphasis is still on management, however. At this level of the organization, a task force oriented toward the user, with participative methods of problem solving, is essential if we are to obtain full commitment to the program.

From systems design, the book moves to a chapter on implementation. We attempt to explain top management's role in pushing for progress to schedule and insisting on high quality of results. The user has the role of debugging and achieving reliance on the new system with a minimum of parallel operation. Proper stress is given to the user's responsibility for and support of data cleanup and the maintenance of data audit reports. We recommend directing implementation toward the areas of larger payoff, since achieving positive results develops increased future support.

The next chapter, on "Living with an MIS System," covers performance in the installation and use of the MIS as well as the overall management of the business in achieving projected profit goals. The best managers get the desired results through the use of the system combined with the "gut-feel" decisions when necessary. It is important to recognize that:

- Too frequently top management does not push for the highest success levels with MIS;

- Too frequently catastrophes have been attributed to living with MIS where, in fact, management, and not the system, is at fault;

- Too frequently results have fallen short of expectations and users have been content to allow them to remain there.

Most of all, management should make the change to MIS exciting and not threatening. This requires the support of people through a period of change, along with praise and reward when the transition has been successfully accomplished.

In the final chapter, I take a look into the future and discuss the impact of success with MIS on all levels of management and labor. We will see great emphasis on central staff work versus separate functional staff; line managers will monitor operations, and assume greater responsibility for expensive equipment. At the same time, we must adjust to a reduction in day-to-day planning by lower levels of management.

The book concludes on a hopeful note—that MIS will increase in both success and impact, that the challenge and benefits will be greater than in the past, and, with participative programs, we can improve "humanism" in business operations.

This book is designed as a training manual as well as a read-through treatise for the professional. The next pages describe the type of participative training recommended. The questions supporting the training practice are placed at the back of each chapter.

Team Development For MIS Support

This book presents a general picture of common (and some not-so-common) problems encountered during the conception, design, and implementation of major industry systems.

From a technical point of view, it includes such issues as:

- Integrating systems across functions,
- Need for realistic accounting systems,
- Considerations in data-base selection and development,
- Data editing and accuracy control,
- Development of a sound master plan, including policy determination, estimation of benefits, and manpower and planning needs over the time space.

It also presents its picture from a *people and a management* point of view. Included here are people being able to work together to solve problems and to plan, managers motivating their subordinates, and people being committed to making the system work.

The reason for this two-part treatment is very simply that *both* areas can cause systems to fail; they can fail because of technical flaws, inadequate designs, or low level of technical skills; they can also fail because the people who should have been prime movers were not involved in the initial phases of the design, and because groups of people from Production Control cannot work with their counterparts in Production because of deep-seated animosities that have never been resolved. As expressed in the design on the cover, their emotions are going in an opposite direction to what is being presented to the intellect. The point is that, since problems that make systems fail can emanate from either the "technical" or the "people" side of organizations (or both), it is important to deal with both when discussing how to recognize and solve systems problems.

In order to enhance the usefulness of this book, we have designed a three-to-five-day workshop for use within companies that have installed, or are about to install, manufacturing systems. The objective of these participative workshops is to enable teams of key people from each functional group involved in the management information system (including, of course, the MIS group itself) to work together in assessing system strengths and weaknesses and in planning for improvement. Typical teams are shown in the table below.

Typical Teams

	Marketing – Sales		Manufacturing – Purchasing			Finance & Cost	Engineering
	Order Entry	Distribution	MRP	Shop-floor control	Purch.	Finance & Cost	Engineering
Systems rep.	X	X	X	X	X	X	X
Sales adm.	X	X	X			X	X
Distribution rep.	X	X	X			Optional	
Manufacturing			X	X	X	X	X
Inventory control	X	X	X	X	X	X	X
Production control			X	X	X	X	Optional
Purchasing	X		X		X	X	X
Cost–Finance	X	X	X	X	X	X	X
Engineering	X		X	Optional	X	X	X

General Process

1. All workshop participants should be furnished copies of this book at least three weeks before the first meeting so that they can read the first two chapters and individually score their company on the score sheet for those chapters. These sheets are specially designed to identify strengths and weaknesses in system logic and performance. These sheets are returned to the consultants and are scored; the important data they provide will be fed back at the beginning of the first workshop, described below.

Prework

- First 2 chapters
- Score company, with questionnaire for first two chapters

Ranking

Depending on the number of factors, the chairperson may wish to compute the average "score" for each—or have the "A's" (most important items) singled out of the list—

- Those closest to 1.0 are facilitators.
- Those closest to 5.0 are hindering.

Meeting I
Day One:

- Introduction
    Expectations
    Objectives
    Agenda

- Feedback—Review of information from individual responses to the questionnaire:

  Strengths, Weaknesses;

  Areas of agreement, areas of disagreement;

  FF, Facilitating factors

  HF, Hindering factors

- Reactions/discussion

Divide into small groups to address problem areas identified in data:
  a) Each group should address itself to each category of problem;
  b) Objectives of each are to expand each category and gain agreement on major hindering and facilitating factors;
  c) Dinner and distribution of prework for Day Two.

Day Two:

- This day will be spent learning the concepts behind and the skills of creative problem solving and teamwork.
- The day (including lectures, exercises, and discussion) will end with each team defining specific action steps to resolve problems identified in Day One.

2. The first meeting lasts two full days and includes all of the team members in a general session with two consultants. The general objectives for this meeting are:
  a) To appraise and reach consensus on the relative ranking of major *facilitating* and *hindering* factors in successful systems (including both those outlined in the book and others that the teams can add on their own).
  b) To recognize, those factors where consensus cannot be reached and either take steps to resolve the differences or reduce the severity of potential impact on progress.
  c) To recognize, within departments and individuals, certain attitudes or management styles that affect cross-functional relationships. Understanding these and, where possible, changing them, will be a significant step toward assuring an excellent system.
  d) To develop and gain commitment to carrying out action steps to improve the major hindering factors.

This meeting is also used to help improve the way in which people work together on the job. Some techniques here include:

- Leading meetings that are efficient and that accomplish objectives;
- Drawing out less active participants;
- Being able to creatively generate alternative problem solutions;
- Enhancing communication and teamwork;
- Gaining consensus on decisions and next steps;
- Critiquing meetings, and offering feedback to assure maximum effectiveness at subsequent meetings.

3. *Action Steps.*

Depending on the time to wrap up the first session—more than one of the items listed above can be subject to action-step development. In some cases, teams may want to schedule extra sessions—time permitting. Experience indicates that there will be some correlation between hindering factors that are developed as the book progresses through:

- Creating a positive environment,
- Development of a system,
- Implementation of the system, and
- Living with the system

Consequently, the Action Program on early items should not be considered frozen until the full workshop has been completed.

4. *Summary.*

At the end of meeting I, each team will have received feedback on system problems, will have identified facilitating and hindering factors to excellent systems, will have set specific action steps to resolve hindering factors, and, most important, will have agreed to each. Each team will also have had the chance to work with counterpart groups, discuss relationship problems openly in a controlled environment, and improve its ability to work as a team. Prework for the next meeting is then selected from the chapters of the book appropriate to the specific group of workshop participants.

Meeting II takes place one week later, and lasts from 1 to 3 days, depending upon the needs of each group. It is at this point that successes and failures of the past week are assessed and analyzed. The teams define areas of improvement and set revised technical and teamwork goals.

Benefits Of This Approach

Our experience shows that it requires a lot of energy, training, and explaining to change an individual's attitude toward a "habit situation." This is true whether you:

Tell them,   Sell them,   Lead them,   Involve them,

in verbal, written, or visual ways, or a combination thereof.

Our experience also shows that it requires geometrically more energy to change a group of 8 (64) than 4 (16) in their attitude towards "habit situations." As the complexity of the development increases, as it does with integrated management-information systems, the success shifts to those who use the

Lead them,   Involve them

approaches. Our workshop method involves a combination of leadership and involvement. Just using involvement without the book would leave many issues unchallenged—some overlooked and some avoided.

With good leadership using the book as guide, management and the company can be evaluated in a thorough way that will frequently bring additional key factors into play.

Where people who work together across functions of the company get their opportunity to "lay it on the line" and then to proceed to a new level of cooperation and improvement, exciting things can happen that will contribute substantially to success in all phases of systems development and implementation.

The questions to be answered by each individual and the group analysis are given at the end of each chapter.

1
Getting Started

Far more computer systems fail because of poor management than because of faulty techniques. While managing an MIS project is admittedly difficult, it can be done provided one knows the different managerial requirements at various stages of the MIS development process. Unfortunately, more attention has been given to the techniques used in Management Information Systems than to the practical managerial requirements for their successful implementation and use.

A. TOWARDS AN MIS PHILOSOPHY

Many top managers wish that the whole subject of MIS and computers would dry up and blow away. To them, the systems area is a headache usually clouded by errors, bickering, and a concern as to whether the company is really getting its money's worth. Usually, the system pot boils in these companies year after year. Unfortunately, there isn't much hope that substantial benefits will be achieved unless there is a drastic change in top management's attitude—for "as ye sow, so shall ye reap."

A smaller number of companies have adopted a *systems philosophy*—"We are going to operate our business through good—if not almost perfect—computer business systems." This requires a lot of attention at first, but pays great dividends later on. This approach involves a systems philosophy with the following key points:

- That complex businesses need complex integrated business systems, and that this network is the nervous and response system of the corporation;

- That the system must be designed and developed to be a servant for the managers.

- That managers must be trained to express their needs and to participate in the design and operation of the system that they want.

- That substantial top function- and division-manager attention is needed at the outset because the network goes across *all* departmental boundaries.

The efficiency with which the system is designed, installed, and operated is directly proportional to the degree of cooperation and commitment at the middle management level.

It is not surprising that the management that supports the MIS philosophy ends up managing through the system, directing it, and not fearing computer dominance. The management that spends money but not time or intelligence in an MIS approach ends up frustrated and hating the "monster"—yet not quite able to do without it. In the former companies, the morale of the systems group and the users is high and they act in a supportive fashion. In the antisystems companies, the morale of system personnel is low and there is much bickering between the users and the systems group.

There is little appreciation of the innumerable things that have to be done almost to 100% perfection to make the system work effectively. Fortunately, in a good system, 85 to 90 percent of the data (once correct) repeats itself with 100 percent reliability.

There is a misapprehension that industry and institutions have been employing computer systems so long that almost everyone is in that "dreamland" and the battle has been won. This is far from true; repeated samples show that only 20 percent of these organizations are operating well at all, and a whopping 80 percent feel they have a long way to go.

There is a risk that managers inadequately committed to MIS will accept modest improvement as good enough, because they have been frustrated by the computer world so long. This book shows the way to raise the percentage of highly successful systems to a new level.

B. DEVELOPMENT OF INFORMATION AND CONTROL SYSTEMS

During the past decade, American industry has seen a revolution in information control. Technological advances in the design of computer hardware and software have opened new opportunities for profit through better control. These advances have drastically reduced the cost of processing data, while greatly increasing the speed of information-handling. Many companies are taking advantage of these new opportunities by moving toward integrated automated-management systems. Some companies have been conspicuously more successful than others. What have been the keys to success in the development of automated information control? To answer this question we should look at five factors that are important to success.

1. A Technological Breakthrough in Control

Prior to World War II, automatic data processing was primarily concerned with reducing the costs of accounting processes. Moreover, information recorded for control purposes was useful only in accounting because of the time lag involved in collecting and processing the data. Even when the introduction of automatic equipment increased the speed of calculations, the accounting emphasis continued. Punch-card and tab-type equipment permitted the handling of multiple types of data, and wired-board programs facilitated its automatic reception and computation with printed results. The 1940's saw an increase in speed and flexibility in handling cards in sequence.

In the early postwar period, more complex wired-board programs made possible the extension of data processing into complete routines. For the first time, whole routines of check-writing, physical inventory, accounts payable and receivable, and payroll, could be mechanized. Still, the fundamental orientation of most operating programs was toward accounting. Indeed, the few firms that ventured into tab (EAM) operations for inventory control, bill-of-material structure, or production control, ran into difficulty, and with reason. Companies have always paid employees and invoiced customers to the accuracy of pennies, and accountants are accustomed to a high level of accuracy. Those companies that attempted nonaccounting applications of automated information control had considerable and, in many cases, unexpected difficulty with the accuracy of their data. The very few firms which stuck to the job of cleaning up these records and procedures saved themselves a lot of time and headaches in later computer applications.

Digital business computers were developed in the early postwar period, but their actual installation on a usable basis did not begin until the middle 50's. The first step from card machines was tape systems. The tape records permitted the storage and processing of data on a sequential batch basis. Programs to service each business function began to increase in complexity.

With the introduction of random-access storage in the late 50's and early 60's, the transfer of data and calculations between records became easier. The flexibility of this external memory device and its related software liberated the computer from its accounting role. The wide range of computer-supported information and control processes applied in manufacturing, engineering, and distribution led to a complete re-evaluation of the role of automation in information and control systems. This rethinking has advanced quite quickly in some companies, while others have been slow to realize that more than clerical labor savings could be achieved from the automated handling of information.

But now, after a decade of experience, most managements expect that the greatest return to the company from the use of data-processing equipment will come from improved controls and better operating results.

Improvements in control have been most significant in these areas:

Statistical Forecasting

The computer has aided in applying exponential smoothing, multiple regression, control limits, and other statistical analyses to thousands of items that cannot be analyzed manually.

Order Entry Systems

Order entry, particularly in companies with many items per order, has always been complicated by the need, after the first pass, for back-ordering, retyping, and re-invoicing. The ability to check availability at initial order entry and the splitting of the back-order immediately has saved both cost and confusion. In addition, the computer generation of customer name and address from customer code numbers, of part specification and prices from part numbers, and automatic credit check, has speeded up the processing and accuracy while reducing the cost of this function.

Computation of Order Quantities

While the computation of EOQ's has been possible for years, the ability to apply this technique to thousands of parts and to maintain changes in the basic data has been improved by the computer.

Computation of Order Signals and Safety Stocks

The use of probability theory to balance stock-out risk and loss of profits against the level of inventory investment is relatively new in application and, again, the computer's ability to handle all of the basic data and to update it is a real benefit.

Price Breaks and Scheduled Purchase Deliveries

"Return on investment" concepts have carried into purchasing, and most companies do not purchase large quantities unless they receive a price break on partial delivery schedules. The computer's ability to handle the detail required to make price-break analyses offers significant cost savings.

EDP and Improvement in Response Lead Time

Lead time is a factor in increasing inventories in all areas, and the time reduction from computer processing reduces inventories accordingly.

Control of Distribution Costs and Reduction of Field Inventories

Optimum costs can be determined by achieving the best balance between transportation, warehouse, and inventory costs, and stock-out risks. It would be virtually impossible to perform the thousands of calculations necessary to determine the optimum mix without a computer, and equally difficult to implement an operating system manually.

Material Requirement Planning Systems

Since 1967 there has been a rapidly increasing development of MRP systems that culminated in a "crusade" for MRP by the American Production and Inventory Control Society in 1972–73. While many of these are not yet (early 1975) fully operative, those that are running have brought about very large reductions in inventory and improvement in performance-to-schedule dates. (See Appendix 2.)

Shop-Floor Control and Priority Scheduling

Shop-floor control systems involve work-center and total input–output balance and control and the application of priority rules to the Queue Lists in each work center. The result, particularly when tied to a net-change MRP system, has been a substantial reduction in work-in-process inventories and the elimination of most of the expediting function.

Master Scheduling and Capacity Planning Systems

Since 1970 Master Scheduling and Capacity Planning Systems have produced savings equally significant to those attributed to MRP. In most cases these systems are fully complementary. While in simpler cases Master Scheduling and Capacity Planning may not require computer programs, most companies will find computer systems beneficial in the long run.

2. Overcoming Managerial Problems in Control

Data problems have been common ever since automated information and control techniques were first applied outside of accounting. Even today, the severity of the data problem is often underestimated. Many managements *talk* about data accuracy, but leave the problem of rooting out inaccuracy to the EDP function, without attempting to identify and correct the real sources of error. Effective data auditing requires coordinated action in four stages. The first is a means of identifying error by cause, quantity, and responsibility. The second step is statistical sampling to provide unbiased information on quality levels and problem areas. Plans for sampling can be tailored to emphasize trouble areas. The third step is a logical process of corrections, at the source, starting with the more crucial items and working toward the less significant. The last step is starting data auditing concurrently with the development of systems and programs.

When tackled by a systematic effort that traces errors to their sources in the functional departments, data problems have proved solvable. Where management has hoped that the system would purge itself of error, little progress has been made. In some cases, errors multiply in an automated system, causing continual disruption, and loss of efficiency, sometimes verging on chaos. The lesson of experience is clear: Quality control in the data center and its input–output operations has become as important as quality control of the product itself.

A second common type of managerial problem lies in the computer operations themselves. While most data problems can be traced to sources outside the EDP function, other failures of computer-supported control programs are due to poor performance of the data center itself.

Many companies have not recognized the changing role of the EDP function in a time of rapid development of control techniques. The data center must both *service* an expanding complex of existing programs and *develop* new and improved programs and systems. Many centers have proved unequal to even the first task alone. Heavy and varied input–output schedules must be maintained, and round-the-clock operation provided. In companies that have not set high standards, the poor performance of the data center, in terms of both time and quality, has adversely affected the attitude of other functions toward expanded use of the computer. Management can no longer afford to think of the data center as another "office operation."

Poor planning of integrated data bases comprise the third major problem area for managers. In poorly managed or badly overloaded data centers, it has proved impossible to do a proper job of planning new computer programs and systems. Companies that have supported thorough planning have made great advances in the integration of automated information and control programs. In the earlier days of computer systems, few companies had the foresight to develop data-base files and integrated programs. Each department made its own demands and was serviced as an independent operation. Basic records were in files that were developed to suit the needs of specific transactions and to produce specific reports. This practice led to considerable duplication, particularly in tape records systems. Companies that developed disk-storage systems gave much more attention to the elimination of duplication, and many did well with the master-part record, sales history, and accounting controls. Few companies, however, did well with product structure, requirements, replenishments, routing, and process detail.

More recently, companies have devoted greater attention to the development of data-base files, where all functions take responsibility for updating information, and each function has programs that operate efficiently from common files.

3. Toward Integrated Business Systems

Thorough planning is making it possible for automated control programs to be linked in a computer-supported business system. In the last few years, a few companies have made progress with integrated EDP systems that lower the operating costs of the function and speed up the response cycle, with greater flexibility to meet changing conditions. These companies have also developed improved techniques in the manufacturing area, including the logistics of production scheduling, priority determination, and workloading. An increasing number of companies are now successfully combining EDP and logistical techniques into an integrated operating system that:

a)   Automates order entry, assigns back orders and invoices, and up-dates forecasting;
b)   Includes Master Scheduling, Capacity Planning and Requirements Planning programs which lead to substantially lower inventories and lower operating costs;
c)   Reduces lead time and improves customer service;
d)   Replaces expediting costs with sound priority rules;
e)   Identifies overtime and excess costs that can be reduced by specific rather than generalized action;
f)   Optimizes distribution costs;
g)   Integrates accounting with operational data.

These advances result in substantial improvement in direct costs and lower indirect operating expenses. Management also has a full knowledge of cause and effect fast enough for the information to be relevant in instituting corrective action. Certainly, a great deal still remains to be done; but systems are presently being planned that will put the optimum management of most complex industries within our grasp. It is now possible for management to consider "total" integrated business systems on a practical basis. We emphasize "practical" since too much time has been spent discussing "total" business systems on a theoretical level. The debate over what makes a system truly "total" is particularly fruitless. Some hold that a system cannot be "total" unless it includes all of the auxiliary subsystems within the company, whether including these makes economic sense or not.

No systems designer would think of placing a Job Shop and a Process Operation under the same system just because they happened to be divisions of the same company. In this case, it would take two "total" systems to provide complete control. It is the practical requirements of each company or division that determine the particular shape that a "total" system will take. What all such systems have in common is that they handle the main business of receiving orders, planning and ordering materials for production, and handling all accounting with personnel, customers, and vendors. We now look at the integrated business system as having four or five primary subsystems:

Order Entry Forecasting, Marketing, Master Scheduling
- Customer order
- Engineering specifications
- Quote
- Forecasting material requirements
- Invoice
- Sales analyses

Material Control (supported by Capacity Planning)
- Requirements planning
- Purchase order

- Bill of material explosion
  (parts lists)
- Inventory
- Requisition

- Receiving ticket
- Accounts payable
- Inventory
- Cost

Production Control

- Inventory
- Operation card
- Man-hours and rate
- Scheduling and
  priority sequencing

- Workloading
- Cost
- Inventory
- Payroll

Distribution (Optional)

- Shipment planning for
  warehouses, branches,
  and customers

- Inventory levels for
  proper service rates,
  control of traffic
  costs, optimum
  rates, etc.

Accounting Control

- Based on cost data
  in the operating systems,
  plus overhead and
  expense analysis

- Gives final cost, in-
  come and balance
  sheet information

Frequently, in the balance of the text, the Main Business System will be used as the focal point of the Management Information System. This approach does not deal with all of the auxiliary systems that might be conceived, because adding such variety would complicate the discussion with little gain to the reader. The Main Business System is that major portion of MIS that all businesses have in common.

4. Planning: The Key to Success

The success enjoyed by a growing number of companies that have fully integrated information and control systems puts pressure on other managements because such companies indicate increased competitiveness and prospects for a better return on investment. These leaders are proceeding with careful thought and guidance, to a greater degree than most companies employed in the early applications of computers. There is a feeling in most of these installations that the job is being done with care and will be highly successful. Doubtless, it is valuable to have some companies risk ideas and reputation in this way, so those who follow in their footsteps will be able to proceed more rapidly and with less fear of failure.

GOALS AND DIRECTIONS

How clear are our goals and directions and to what degree are people committed to them. . .

Planning requires both setting of clear goals and directions and the communication of these to all levels of management.

No management can afford to adopt a "wait and see" attitude, however. The lessons of the past ten years are clear: Success comes to those who plan broadly and thoroughly. Companies that plunged into computerization without an integrated plan have found it difficult and expensive to bring order out of the proliferation of programs. Particularly vulnerable are those companies whose EDP function has attempted to prove that it can cater to the special whims of each department. The management of one large company that began computerization when this approach seemed reasonable found itself, several years later, presiding over a welter of *1200 different programs*. A comprehensive analysis of this nearly unmanageable situation indicated that a set of 200 programs operating from data-base files would do a better job. But how to get there? The road of reorganization has not been an easy one. By the painful consolidation of approximately 100 programs a year, management will arrive at their desired goal in about ten years. Ten years of retreat to achieve what a carefully worked out implementation plan can achieve in five, building from scratch! Certainly no company wants to repeat this costly and trying process.

Yet, tragically, some managers pursue a segmented approach today. Many of these managers have directed the successful development of

> # MISDIRECTED ENERGY
> # IS
> # ORGANIZED
> # WRONGHEADEDNESS

new products, but they fail to recognize that the development and introduction of expanded computer programs and systems requires similar care. In both areas there must be plans, model development, tests, redesigns, and sales. Master planning schedules have to be made and maintained. Resources and funds have to be committed and progress checked against milestones. Evaluations lead to a reassignment of resources and adjustments of schedules. The manager must be concerned that the product is usable, that it won't need basic redesign soon, that it is flexible and adaptable to meet new needs. Managers who have been successful with integrated business systems have recognized these similarities and insisted on following an orderly plan which:

a)   made sure that the line and staff managers wanted the outputs of the integrated system,
b)   was based on an integrated design that avoided costly duplication,
c)   monitored performance during development and programming,
d)   included rigorous testing and debugging before "customer" exposure, and
e)   included sufficient time and effort to train personnel in how to use the system.

5. Need for Realistic Accounting Systems

A popular myth of management is that current absorption-cost systems will be adequate for managerial control once the data is made accurate and the MIS system is functioning. In no other area of professional activity has so much time produced such poor or misleading results. Consider the following: The XYZ Company, with a good MIS system, was selling two grades of its product to a major customer. A competitor, operating on about the same schedule, suggested taking all one grade and giving XYZ the other. The sales volume of XYZ remained the same, but the company lost a million dollars of profit because of the poor marginal income on the grade it retained.

Accounting systems are the weakest portion of most business systems. This is not only because of an almost blind adherence to absorption costing but also a variety of weak practices. One example is that most systems charge the cost of purchasing, receiving, inspecting, handling, and storing of both components and materials entirely to manufacturing overhead, which distorts "make or buy" decisions as well as some product margins. Most systems also calculate poorly, if at all, the proper value of products produced on numerical-control machine tools, high-speed presses, and other multipurpose equipment, as compared to the costs by single-purpose, slow equipment.

Yet another example is that few systems properly treat the overhead cost of engineering and sales on new products versus old, or the overhead charges on spare parts versus new assemblies. Few systems properly charge fixed or period costs to the product involved; most use only a direct labor base, and few systems properly split fixed and variable expenses so that cost changes can be estimated for changes in product volume of ±25 percent.

All of these problems can be corrected by direct cost systems, many of which are operating successfully today.

6. What's Ahead in the Book

It is one problem to forecast the future and quite another to plan the actual transition from present to future. Through discussion of the experience of many of our industrial businesses with computer-supported control systems, this book will help management tackle the major organizational changes which that transition will require. It is our belief that, with the proper master planning, it is possible to extract full profit potential from new control tools and techniques while avoiding pitfalls and out-of-control situations. What are the essential elements of successful planning for an integrated information and physical control system?

Until recently, the term "feasibility study" encompassed the planning of work related to computerized operations. In most cases, these studies were too hardware-oriented. Since failures and delays came largely from other areas, managers become increasingly disappointed in this approach. Other companies, by contrast, seemed to know where they were going and generally expressed satisfaction with their rate of accomplishment. These companies had surveyed broadly, reconciled major differences between functions, and appraised more carefully the requirements for systems design, programming, management education, and data auditing than had those that employed the typical feasibility study.

This broader planning approach, known as the Master Plan (or sometimes the Horizon or Overview Plan), places more emphasis on the effect of computerization on operating performance in terms of both profits and customer service. The integration between functions and the practical needs of each area are given primary emphasis in the systems design. Such a planning program includes five stages, each of which is represented by a chapter of this book: Preparing Top Management for a Key Role in MIS, Creating a Positive Environment for Change, Designing the System, Implementing an MIS System, and Living with an MIS System.

The magnitude of the changes confronting industry are a serious challenge to today's top management. In the past, obsolescence was a problem that could usually be solved. Product development, backed by heavy funding, could usually restore competitiveness of design to a company's products unless sweeping technological changes required diversification into other products altogether. Similarly, when management discouraged the risks associated with change and made adherence to obsolete procedures mandatory, a significant change in top leadership and a substantial amount of re-education could usually salvage the company. Of course, it is never easy to introduce a capability for managing change into an environment where "not making a mistake" means "do it as it always has been done"—right or wrong. Sometimes consultants have been used to bring in new programs or systems not worthy of the attention accorded them, to provide a rallying point around which people could bring justification for a break with old habits.

Recovery from managerial obsolescence in the computer age will not be as easy as it has been in the past, because of the increased tempo of operations and the enormous organizational and technological complexity of the changes that must be made. In this light, the failure of many managements to face up to the future is serious. Especially vulnerable are those of the "Run-the-business-by-the-seat-of-your-pants-with-a-minimum-of-overhead-staff" school, who will often delight the financial world which can make outstanding profits on the short run. The "seat of the pants" proponents fail to recognize that the serious ongoing study of computer applications is not "fat" or inefficiency but a key to continued competitiveness. At the other extreme, those managements too cumbersome to manage sweeping changes are also in a perilous position. Managers in a billion-dollar corporation recently told us: "Take your reference about straightening out our part-number problem and cleaning up our bills of material out of your proposal. Our top management would be too frightened by the magnitude of such a task. Let's work on some fringe areas where we can show some quick results." This ostrichlike approach is dangerous: It amounts to a failure to face up to the fundamental changes required by a truly integrated control system. Such failures prolong costly inefficiencies and leave the company vulnerable to out-of-control situations.

Both of these situations are examples of the "emotion" opposing the "intellect." In the seat-of-the-pants operations, divisional and functional executives are "results-oriented" for their own responsibilities and not likely to want to interface with others. Their "emotions" are centered on the scope and prerogatives of their functions regardless of the soundness of the intellectual approach of the MIS staff. In the second case the emotion of the managers to avoid a major crisis was in conflict with the intellect over the facts of what should be done, and emotion won again. If large corporations cannot adjust to meet these demands, then the pressure to make successful computer applications may bring about more independent divisions.

Nearly everyone recognizes that the demand upon management during a period of change is a multiple of that required in a stable situation. What has perhaps not been recognized fully is that, in today's world of rapid change brought about by the introduction of computer-based information systems, we may need more dynamic managers and fewer static managers in our industrial businesses.

QUESTIONS

(In addition to the teams' ranking, some actual checking of factual data should be done)

1. How do you compare our company's progress in EDP systems in the following areas?

	Poor	Slow	Average	Good	Excellent	Superior
Marketing						
Manufacturing						
Material Cost						
Purchasing						
Finance						
Engineering						
Distribution						
Personnel						
Total						

QUESTIONS—Continued

2. How do you rank our company's progress on Data Accuracy?

	Poor	Slow	Average	Good	Excellent	Superior
Cycle to computer stock status						
Cycle counts to work-in-process						
Transaction error rate						

3. How does our company's management rate in planning EDP systems?
   ☐ Poor   ☐ Fair   ☐ Average   ☐ Good   ☐ Excellent   ☐ Superior

4. How good is our company's accounting system?

	Poor	Fair	Average	Good	Excellent	Superior
Profit or marginal contributions by product line						
Variances to standard for:						
Volume						
Materials						
Labor						
Overhead						

2
Preparing Top Management For A Key Role in MIS

A. ANALYZING TOP MANAGEMENT AND DEVELOPING
AN APPROPRIATE APPROACH
B. SURVEY OF POTENTIAL AND MASTER
PLAN DEVELOPMENT
C. EVALUATING THE LEADERSHIP ROLE
D. PROBLEMS IN
CROSSING FUNCTIONAL LINES
E. SEEKING FULL POTENTIAL AND
BEING PROFIT-ORIENTED

Another current myth is that most top managers and users can't take the responsibility for the Master Plan; rather, they have a sense of timing that "gets things accomplished at the right time." No one will argue that there are some key executives, perhaps 25 percent, who do not lead programs of improvement or develop master plans for implementing major efforts; no one will argue that a sense of timing or opportunity is not important; and no one will argue that management-by-exception is not a sound principle.

Consultants, however, will argue that most major corporate changes are carried out under planned programs involving many parallel and related activities. In most instances, such changes are inspired, directed, and controlled by top management—and carried out through the users. With Management Information Systems there are both the EDP groups and the users, which complicates the change process.

Top management is the key for a successful MIS program. The first step is to determine the extent to which top management is likely to assume its leadership role in MIS. The purpose of this chapter is to explore ways and means of assuring top-management involvement and of launching an MIS program.

Analyzing top management and developing an appropriate approach is essential, particularly if top management is not both well informed on MIS and action-oriented. The MIS sponsor should obtain funds to survey potential costs, savings, and benefits, and to develop a master plan. After a Survey of Potential and Master Plan Development, this chapter takes up the Leadership Role. Rarely, does a change affect so many interfunctional roles as does MIS, and a discussion of Crossing Functional Lines comes next. The chapter concludes on a note of *Going after the Full Potential and Being Profit Oriented;* too few companies, even those with good MIS systems, achieve the maximum benefits possible.

A. ANALYZING TOP MANAGEMENT AND DEVELOPING AN APPROPRIATE APPROACH

The manager who undertakes to develop an MIS program to present to top management must know his audience. Managements vary tremendously in their knowledge of and attitudes toward Management Information Systems, and the originator of a successful program must fit his approach to the backgrounds and attitudes encountered. Managements can be categorized in several general groups.

1. Well Informed and Action-Oriented

These top people, by virtue of their background and systems-assimilation capabilities, can understand Management Information Systems in concept and implementation. They probably have had experience with companies that were well ahead of the average. They lead the program and require no selling, except possibly on the amount of education and time required to help less informed people understand and operate the system.

We find that the informed, action-oriented group seeks assistance to review programs for omissions or poor estimates. They want monitoring of progress and assistance, if justified by savings, in improving the time schedule. Only occasionally does this group ask for a "cost-justification study;" either they have completed it themselves or they are convinced the savings far exceed the investment. They also believe that the MIS will bring intangible improvements—more potential of using data, tighter control, enhanced training of personnel.

2. Well Informed

Occasionally we see a well-designed MIS system that has been running in parallel with the old system for several years: nothing wrong in concept, but little right in actual use. In less open managements, the extent of the use of the new MIS system may be cleverly disguised at the lower levels. Action orientation is missing. This group needs someone to continually critique progress, to schedule, and to advise and educate line managers in a meaningful way. Consulting is worthwhile in this environment, particularly if it can be combined with the internal, action-oriented people below the chief executive. The MIS manager must build into his program tight progress-reporting procedures and a formal review procedure that involves top management. After implementation, extensive checks and audits must be an integral part of the system.

3. Partially Informed, Action-Oriented

Here the MIS manager must cope with competition from other attention-getters. If the boss believes more is to be achieved by increased sales effort, introduction of new products, and labor and material control, rather than MIS, he may not take the time to learn enough about MIS to change his mind. Often a simulation (manual or computer), demonstrating how decisions could be made and operations carried out under MIS, will help obtain the support required. Unfortunately, many computer experts have moaned that MIS does not offer the opportunity for cost-savings appraisal because such savings cannot be measured by the old "manpower-replacement yardstick" found in the traditional accounting applications. Plant visits to companies where success has been achieved, and talks with the management directly involved in MIS programs, are particularly meaningful to this type of management. Once convinced, thee action-oriented type of executive may approve, study further, and support the MIS program.

4. Partially Informed, Delegative Type

This group cannot successfully carry out an MIS program. Lack of knowledge, coupled with a large amount of delegation to subordinates, creates an environment that stimulates arguments and roadblocks whenever MIS is proposed. It is best to proceed on a piecemeal basis and aim toward limited objectives and short-term improvement.

The partially informed, not action-oriented executive classification forms one of the biggest groups of managers today. They understand enough about MIS to want all of the benefits, but care little for any of the pains. They are also particularly concerned about the costs and failures that have occurred in other companies. Unfortunately, those who are afraid of, or those who wish to delay, MIS can use this top-management attitude as a "shield" for lack of interest, support, and cooperation. Programs become bogged down in delays or are underfunded, as a result. The best approach for the active insiders and outsiders is to team up to force issues toward clearcut resolution: either progress forward to an actively supported program, or a retreat to a lower-cost, piecemeal, service approach.

5. Disinterested, Action-Oriented

These people like improvement and desire change; they tend to prefer less complex tools than MIS because they can control the implementation more effectively and get results in a shorter period of time. They tend to be somewhat afraid of MIS, partly because of lack of knowledge, partly because successful implementation requires a greater degree of involvement and of dependence upon others than do ongoing programs.

The disinterested action-oriented executive is worth convincing, because once he or she is committed, the results will be excellent. The failure to convince stems from the reluctance of these executives to involve others to the degree required by an MIS system. These men or women typically voice antagonism toward computers and staff people in general, preferring to react directly to problems. Staff people and computers are regarded as "necessary evils." Perhaps the only way to convince such men is through the success of those they respect who have seen the benefits of MIS.

6. Disinterested

There are executives who "retire" when they reach the top spot. To them, change is threatening, errors are bothersome. Immediate profits may be more enhanced by "stinginess" than by action. It would be risky to try MIS within this environment. Those companies who have tried, perhaps because of an aggressive person in the middle, usually failed.

This group of disinterested, not action-oriented, top management is also large. It is probably a waste of time to try to sell such a group. The subordinate involved had best change his job, and the Board involved should eventually change its Chief.

Thus, convincing top management depends on the type of management involved. For the companies where there is hope of proving a potential return, cost justification studies and visits to other plants may help pave the way. One- to three-day orientation seminars that cover the top manager's role sometimes start the self-appraisal that leads to success. We take up the cost-justification studies and the development of a master plan next, because with all but the "well informed, action-oriented," a cost justification may be needed in order to secure the support of the MIS plan.

B. SURVEY OF POTENTIAL AND MASTER PLAN DEVELOPMENT

The major items in a survey cover not only savings and costs, but also the difficulties of accomplishing the objective. A survey that projects the goals and faces the problems, keeps management from losing its way or quitting early because of disappointment. The plan should cover both short- and long-range activities. All too frequently, only the long-range programs are considered; and the company suffers short-term systems and operational problems while waiting three or four years for complete MIS implementation. If attention is given to immediate improvements at the outset, attitudes are better during MIS installation, and some profit improvements may offset some or all of the installation costs.

The size and scope of the survey will vary from company to company, but every survey has certain common elements.

1. The survey report should be aimed at top management and should be in sufficient depth to enable them to make the decision to proceed to system design.

2. The survey should include a review of all company policies that may be affected by MIS. The objective, among other things, is to keep top management involved.

3. The survey should include a schedule of estimated costs and benefits. The schedule should be time-phased, showing costs versus savings (monthly or quarterly) throughout the project. The ability to review this schedule at regular intervals provides another method of keeping top management involved.

4. A Master Plan should be developed, one that is directly related to the schedule of costs and benefits. It should identify major milestones in the course of the project, which in turn dictate when top management reviews should occur. A PERT network is a convenient device

for displaying the Master Plan. The critical points, which have nothing to do with techniques, are:

a) The Plan must be followed.
b) The Plan must be dynamic, allowing for the fact that things seldom happen as we expect them to.
c) The Plan, and progress in meeting it, must be updated and reviewed regularly.

5. The survey may include a Macro (or Horizon) Plan, or Overview System Design (if not, this should be one of the first steps in the Master Plan). The Macro System Design describes the general concepts to be implemented in the MIS. It specifies what the various subsystems are, how they relate to one another, and, to a limited extent, what techniques will be used to make them work. Perhaps the best way to describe the Macro System Design is "This is the way we want to run the operating details of the company."*

C. EVALUATING THE LEADERSHIP ROLE

Another myth is that the computer world is so complex that top management cannot comprehend it, which forces them to rely blindly on specialists. No top manager is expected to have complete expertise in *any* specific staff skill. He merely needs to be knowledgeable enough to approve or modify major programs and to maintain balance in corporate efforts. Properly instructed, top managers can learn enough about the computer in a day, and about management information systems in three days more, to participate in the discussions involved. Once the door is open, the balance of the education comes principally from direct association with various computer applications.

Let's assume we have made it this far. We have convinced top management that MIS is a worthwhile program of high return; we have completed the survey, and we have developed the Master Plan. The next step is to look at the leadership requirements for continued success. From the outset, leadership in MIS is important at three different levels of the organization, each making its own contribution.

1. The Chief Executive

All of the functions affected by MIS report to the chief executive (or his senior officer delegate). This could be the Chairman, President, Executive Vice President, or Vice President of a wholly independent division. The time and support he should give to MIS varies with the stage of development of the program, but it is heaviest at the time of:

---

*A five year Master plan has existed (with subsequent revisions) at Nordberg since 1968-See Appendix 2.

a) Planning and policy formation,
b) Systems approval, and
c) Final installation support.

2. The Steering Committee

If the steering committee is regarded solely as a peace-making device, as it often is, the program will fall far short of objectives. Functional executives on the steering committee have to show interest and insist on aggressive progress in their own functions. Frequently, the second-in-command from the various functions make up the part or full-time task force that the MIS leader directs. This helps to improve communications.

The steering committee is the top group that can benefit from Organization Development workshop training and participation. The task forces and application groups also should have appropriately designed programs. These are further described in chapter 3.

3. Task Force Leader

Nothing makes up for a poor colonel—so the saying goes. The task-force leader should have substantial experience in EDP and systems, as well as in operatons, but most of all the ability to *maintain perspective* over changes in all areas of the business. This person should be an excellent manager and salesman and experienced in carrying out major changes successfully. In almost all cases, it is best that this person not be the EDP–MIS Manager. (Occasionally in smaller companies there is no other acceptable choice.)

D. PROBLEMS IN CROSSING FUNCTIONAL LINES

Another myth is that all you need is top management's blessing of the MIS application, since lower levels of systems, EDP, and other line and staff people do all the required work. While not minimizing the importance of the detail work, the two most significant factors in success frequently are overlooked.

First, there may be policy and organization changes that are the direct concern of top management. Second, the basic conceptual design of the system must reflect accurately the nature of the business and the manner in which *top management* wishes to run that business. Neither of these responsibilities can be delegated, and the failure of top management to recognize its critical role in MIS is perhaps the most dangerous threat of all.

The most serious problem facing the chief executive is developing positive support and coordination of key functional subordinates. This is a two-factor problem. Sometimes a functional manager pledges nominal support, but fails to direct his or her subordinates to participate in the planning and implementation of an integrated system. Functional managers cannot assume that cooperation from their subordinates in routine day-to-day matters is automatically extended to planning changes, because lower levels of management are more likely to regard changes as threatening, and particularly so if approval of the change is not made obvious from above.

A functional manager who really supports the chief executive on MIS installation and wants his or her function to do all that is required should give continued positive support, checking frequently at lower levels to be sure that the MIS program is understood and is being carried out. Unfortunately, some functional and divisional executives spar for power over the system and merely give lip-service support to the program. The most difficult manager to deal with is the one who verbally agrees to the program but plays a game of passive resistance to progress, which is reflected down through his or her section of the company.

E. SEEKING FULL POTENTIAL AND BEING PROFIT-ORIENTED

1. Push for Complete Reliance on and Use of the System

The final area in preparing top management is to look beyond the immediate MIS application and compare the company that moves ahead to one that remains dormant.

Perhaps the best way to visualize the benefits is to visit places where the installation of MIS is well advanced. Here management can speculate more accurately on further improvements that can be made. In one situation we studied, a general manager forcibly continued the automation of an inventory, shop order, scheduling, and expediting system that originally required ten men to operate—finally reaching the point where it became a one-man monitoring operation. This reduction was far more dramatic than anything we have experienced elsewhere.

In another case, a company was confronted with a five-month strike, but the computer-based business was fully operated by a skeleton crew. Expedite lists, job location, and maintenance of inventory reservations and balances permitted the company to ship at three-quarters of the normal volume, by having other staff people run machines. When the strike was over, the control system was up to date and had not suffered in relation to shop status. The factory manager said, "Without the computer system, such results could never have been achieved—we would have been dead in the water."

By contrast, those managers who remain in a manual mode, or at most employ segmented EDP programs, are creating a serious gap that must be bridged before reaching the integrated systems world. While the time required to design and develop programs in the future may be reduced by technical advances, this is of little consolation when one realizes how serious is the loss of the education and practical experience that could have been developed during the installation period.

There is danger in a "Pollyanna" attitude, however; things do not work out right unless substantial attention is given to detail. Progress has to be audited continuously from several viewpoints:

a)   Systems design.
b)   Data preparation and accuracy.
c)   Time expended.
d)   Cost expended.
e)   Involvement and attitude of user personnel.

2. The Difficult Job Shops Take Longer

Another myth blindly accepted is the concept that mass-production industries have the most to gain from computer applications. In the past, certainly, it has been true that the automated control of production has been more extensive in mass or process industries. But integrated information and control systems are now being designed for job shops and semi-mass-production industries as well. Because of the complexities involved in these industries, the return on investment is far greater there than in the mass production areas. New software, such as Bill of Material Processors, Material Requirement Planning Systems, and Scheduling and Workloading Programs, make job-shop systems feasible; now we need to train management so that it is capable of developing and implementing these technological advances.

Job-shop MIS installations require both a more complex design and a more difficult data clean-up than most industries. On balance, the percentage savings are far more attractive too. Unfortunately, the techniques involved require a higher degree of practical understanding, which is hard to get in a job-shop environment.

The biggest problems of job-shop operations are Master Scheduling of facilities, the control of released workloads, shipping on schedule, and the control of inventories. Fortunately, manual methods permit substantial improvement in Master Scheduling. Progress in this area frequently leads to management support for the control of "A" items. ("A" items have been categorized separately from "B" and "C" items, because the "A's" cover the small percentage of items that have the biggest (60–80%) impact on the result. The more numberous B and C items obviously have far less impact in total and on a per item basis as well. This principle of Maldistribution was discovered by Alfredo Pareto and has been applied to inventory values, quality losses, and purchase and manufacturing piece costs.) A demonstration that control of a small percentage of expensive items can produce meaningful results in both scheduling and inventory reduction may lead to support for the whole MIS program. Most job-shop managers are very pragmatic: They don't appreciate a long-winded theoretical presentation, but they are ready to accept things on the basis of practical demonstration.

3. Keep the Program Under Control

A "dynamic" attitude backed by confidence and control permits management and staff to roll with the punches and this will prevent covering up misfortune. Good control forces into the open issues that otherwise get missed. (One manager commented, not quite facetiously, "Don't ever throw the PERT chart away and transfer to a new one—I'd lose control—just add another sheet if necessary.") The result of proper control is on-time performance because managers are forced to appraise troublesome situations earlier, add resources, and make timely decisions.

These two factors are fundamental: Without confidence, company personnel cannot tolerate changes and criticism and, without control, confidence will be lost.

It is important to avoid out-of-control situations that lead to heavy cost for "fire-fighting." Typically management employs expeditors and spends overtime dollars to compensate for the lack of good planning and control. This is disorganized wrongheadedness. Unfortunately, the "fire-fighting" style seems attractive because it seems to show movement and get results. This gaining acceptance for a planning style has both an emotional and intellectual side.

UNDIRECTED ENERGY
IS
DISORGANIZED
WRONGHEADEDNESS

4. Watch the Profit Plan All the Way

Why have some companies profited as the MIS system was implemented and run close to their cost and time estimates, while other companies have done so poorly? Perhaps the most important difference is simply that the chief executive insists on having it that way, and in so doing he also requires his staff to:

a) Get interim improvements at the outset.
b) *Use* the system as it develops.
c) Provide ample communication and discussion meetings involving all key people.
d) Have a good cost-reduction study.
e) Maintain control of business.
f) Make up behind-schedule conditions and maintain good manning.

ALIGN

LACK OF ALIGNMENT CREATES ORGANIZATIONAL ENERGY CRISIS

Misdirected Energy
Undirected Energy

Planning effectively and operating to plan aligns energies so that the MIS program moves forward and leads to a superior MIS installation.

F. SUMMARY

Five items of major significance have evolved over the past four years in the successful development of computer information systems.

1. The importance of a Steering Committee task force in integrating the organization, achieving user involvement and integrating different disciplines.

2.   The importance of data-base files in eliminating both file and program duplication and proliferation.

3.   Understanding the significant use of the "main business system."

4.   The necessity of data auditing and data improvement.

5.   The tremendous need for a Master Plan of implementation, spelling out resources (men and materials) and timetables. The emphasis in these plans is on aiding in more profitable operations.

Task forces are important, but they need the best people as members. The use of Organization Development techniques to gain user participation in the detailed development and implementation of the system has been very successful.

The factors established in the old Hawthorne experiments years ago are still valid and important: When one participates in a program that *management* deems important, the program is successful. Top managements who delegate responsibility for EDP systems because these are too technical contribute to a failure syndrome.

QUESTIONS

1.   Top Management's Attitude towards MIS

	Closest fit	Next closest fit
Well informed and action-oriented		
Well informed		
Partially informed, action-oriented		
Partially informed, delegative		
Disinterested, action-oriented		
Disinterested		
Other		

QUESTIONS—Continued

2. Potential benefits of EDP Systems
   (Please estimate these
   the best you can.)

	$ improvements		
	Accom-plished	in devel-opment	future plans
Forecasting			
Customer service			
Engineering support			
Quality control			
Inventory reduction			
Productivity			
Cost control			

How much could be saved if we could operate at the best level possible?

3. How well is your company organized to be successful with EDP systems?

	Poor	Slow	Average	Good	Excellent	Superior
Commitment of chief executive						
Steering committee from functions						
Excellent task-force leaders						
Ease of crossing functional lines						

4. Is your company ready to push for a system you can rely upon?

	Poor	Slow	Average	Good	Excellent	Superior

(This means an intent to *replace* the existing method, not just try out the new and use it if it is O.K.)

5. If you have a complex change, have you allowed enough time and training?

6. How committed is management to maintaining control before, during, and after a major systems change?

(This means an intent to *replace* the existing method, not just try out the new and use it if it is O.K.)

3
Creating a Positive Environment for Change

A. INTRODUCTION: THE HUMAN SIDE OF MANAGEMENT SYSTEMS

In the course of implementing a succession of actual industrial applications of computer-based business systems, we continually blend a growing reservoir of experience with fresh ideas to meet the peculiar needs of each new situation. Competitive management in the computer age requires a combination of determination to carry out a comprehensive program, coupled with an insistence on "making do" with the current state of development of systems. We cannot wait for all possible new discoveries to be made before we decide to proceed.

In every installation, hindsight points to methods, techniques, and controls that could have been handled in a better way. Most frequently, they can be seen more clearly after various subsystems are linked together and begin to provide the daily, weekly, monthly, and special operating routines for running the business. It is equally important to recognize that not every opportunity for optimization can be envisioned at the start of the project, and that improvements will be found along the way.

Management should be concerned with the often subconscious tendency to delight in the imperfections of both the computer business system and the data within it. This is part of the "organizational climate" which affects the success of all changes contemplated by the company. This may even reflect a hope that the current structure and system *cannot* be changed. In contrast, a few instances show what can be achieved when a positive environment for change does exist. The chief executive and his key managers set the framework within which the organizational climate develops. If risk-taking and actively supporting change is applauded and rewarded more than "being right by doing it the old way," the negative forces will be minimal.

In most of the cases, the MIS installations had the active support of the chief executive. Even in one that did not have such support, there was sufficient counterbalancing power to keep the program from failure (though the delaying effect was substantial). In a billion-dollar company the program had the active support of both the divisional president and the corporate financial vice president. In so large a company, it was difficult for men even as powerful as these to accelerate the rate of change.

In spite of the critical tone we take in analyzing the various pitfalls uncovered, most of the programs discussed herein can be considered successful or on the road to success. Some may have missed the time-performance objectives, or could have been substantially more effective during the transition period; but the final MIS development was several steps ahead of what existed before.

At the time of application, many of these cases were at the forefront of business systems development, and there was little to learn from

ORGANIZATION CLIMATE

That combination of factors that makes up the ¨emotional environment¨ within which people work. . .

others. Far more intuition than experience went into the creation of their computer systems. Later, as computer applications spread in a variety of industries, some of the expected major problems become more pronounced, while others are diminishing. Several years ago, most professionals would have outlined the problems as:

1. Training of competent people,
2. ˙ Capability of equipment,
3. Accuracy or quality of data, and
4. Overemphasis on accounting applications.

While these problems are still with us, others are now assuming greater importance. The major problems coming to the surface are psychological—a combination of people's attitude toward change *per* se, and their ability to work together effectively to institute change.

It is a mistake to assume that the personnel of the strong line functions of a business have a natural tendency to cooperate. It is a greater mistake to assume such cooperation during the major changes involved when installing an integrated management information system.*

---

*"The Human Side of Management Systems," *Business Automation,* November 1968, by Arnold O. Putnam, Rath & Strong, Inc.

There is also substantial evidence that the larger the company, the less the cooperation, since the distance from the head to the lowest level increases with the size of the company. In a bureaucratic organization, coordination across the lower functional levels is that much more difficult to obtain when changes have to go higher for executive approval within each function. When people are asked to cooperate on the routine conduct of business, they develop habit performance patterns, but when they are asked to cooperate during a time of change in their own routines, many questions and insecurities arise:

1. How will this affect me?
2. Personally, will I be better off with the success or failure of the change?
3. Shouldn't my greatest loyalty be to my own function?
4. Shouldn't I get credit for all or part of a modified new proposal?
5. Would my stature look better if that of the others looks worse?
6. In this time of change, shouldn't I get a bigger job?
7. Why should I do the extra work when the new and the old systems run in parallel?
8. If I keep the old system accurately, won't the new look less attractive?
9. If new information highlights problems that I know exist so that they become visible to my boss, will they blame me?
10. Will I lose control in the conversion stage if problems arise that cannot be solved quickly?

These questions are both logical and emotional and have to be dealt with if change is to be accomplished successfully.

With all of these and more questions being explored at many levels of the organization, is it any surprise that MIS installations run into difficulty? A technique that appraises the Organizational Climate as well as the attitudes in regard to many of these questions is called MAPPING. It is described in the section that follows.

B. MAPPING

A good method to appraise the human attitude and technical status is to make a map. Mapping* assesses the present status of an organization relative to its potential, to determine in which resources major oppor-

---

*Mapping is a part of Rath & Stong's Force Three approach to making companies outstanding. It usually follows a Motion Study and a Competitive Edge Program. Mapping can be successfully used in any area. A multi-disciplinary approach is essential to success. See Appendix 1.

ORGANIZATION EFFECTIVENESS

diagnoses of both
LOGICAL and EMOTIONAL
sides of the management
of each function in the
organization

---

tunities for improvement exist. The analysis and diagnosis is unique in that it provides a picture (or map) of major functions along two dimensions:

a) The efficiency of employment of physical, technical, and financial resources (resource efficiency), and
b) The effectiveness of the organization in managing its human resources (organization effectiveness).

The Mapping stage has these objectives:

• To gather, analyze, and feed back information relative to both resource efficiency and organization effectiveness, so that the organization can pinpoint strengths and areas that need to be improved.

• To involve people throughout the organization in gathering and analyzing information.

• To combine the skills, viewpoints, and technologies of people throughout the company to provide a truly objective and comprehensive picture of the organization.

• To provide sufficient data to organizational leaders so that accurate, high-quality, and knowledgeable decisions can be made, and plans for the future can be developed.

1. What is a Map?

A MAP (or Management Action Picture) is a profile that graphically displays the gap between the actual and the optimal levels of performance in the use of key resources by a department, functional unit, or total organization. It is composed of two axes, or dimensions, as shown in Fig. 3.1 The horizontal dimension is termed *Resource Efficiency* (RE) and assesses the current status and potential of physical, financial, and technical resources. The vertical dimension, *Organization Effectiveness*

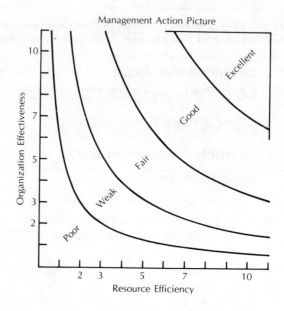

Figure 3.1

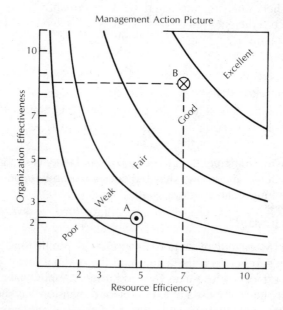

Figure 3.2

(OE), is designed to diagnose the human equation of the organization and determine the emotional, interpersonal, and organization factors that could help or hinder goal achievement.

Data are gathered along both of these axes and analyzed so that they can be plotted on the MAP. Figure 3.2 shows a sample MAP of a production department of a major United States manufacturer. Point A represents the current status of this department's effective utilization of both its human and its technical resources. Point B shows the level that functional managers and top management currently see as the goal—the point at which they feel the department should be along both OE and RE dimensions.

Point A is an assessment of the current level of organizational effectiveness and resource efficiency.

Point B, then, indicates the level that people in this department are seeking to achieve, based upon directions from department heads, managers at higher levels, or their own desires (supporting data to the MAP, in fact, would indicate which of these options plays the most significant part). It is also a result of meetings with department members and consultants to explore the possibility and desirability of different goals. The purpose is not for the consultants to set goals for the client but, rather, to probe the limits of possibility and cost effectiveness and to draw upon experience in other situations to ask, "Have you considered . . .?" or "What about trying . . .?" Point B, then, is determined by the people in the department as a result of meeting with the consultants.

2. What is Included
in the Resource Efficiency Dimension?

The Resource Efficiency (RE) dimension of the MAP is designed to measure how efficiently the physical, financial, and technical resources of the organization are being utilized. Areas of diagnosis obviously differ depending on which particular resources are employed in a specific function or organization. The table on the following page describes some typical areas that could be included in questionnaires under Resource Efficiency in a mapping project in a manufacturing organization for the Marketing and Purchasing functions. The items below represent sample areas of investigation in each of the corresponding functions in the column on the left.

The functions of Research & Development, Manufacturing, Engineering, and Personnel are not detailed here. In addition to internal data, mapping also encompasses a number of industry yardsticks that offer valuable industrywide comparison. Some of these indicators are:

- Inventory Turnovers vs. Industry Average
- ROI vs. Industry Average
- Shipment and Performance vs. Industry Average
- Sales $/Salesman vs. Industry Average
- Profit on Sales vs. Industry Average
- Value of Shipments per man-hours (or wage dollar) vs. Industry Average
- Productivity vs. Industry or Daywork or Measured Daywork
- Total Quality Cost vs. Industry Average
- Capital Investment per employee vs. Industry Average

Table 3.1 Areas of Investigation for Assessment of Resource Efficiency in Marketing and Purchasing.

Marketing	Market knowledge
	Product characteristics
	Sales planning
	Sales control
	Forecasting
	Sales management and organization
	Customer relations
	Pricing policies and procedures
	Advertising and promotion
	Distribution
Purchasing	Effectiveness of control system
	Ability to gain best possible prices
	Knowledge and control of vendors
	Quality of communication with other departments
Production and Inventory Planning and Control	Order entry
	Item control
	Inventory planning
	Resource planning
	Production control
Financial	Financing
	Profitability
	Financial accounting
	Inventory valuation
	Cost accounting and control
Quality Assurance	Organization
	Information system
	Practices

3. What is Included in the Organization Effectiveness Dimension?

The purpose of the MAP's Organization Effectiveness dimension is to diagnose and measure the various dynamics of the organization and its management. It also determines probable root causes of trouble and analyzes their impact upon the human (as opposed to the physical, financial, and technical) resources of the organization. The purpose is not to make judgments but, rather, to present an objective picture of the data that exist and that are either helping or hindering the organization in being effective and in achieving its goals. It is only with this type of data, combined with that gathered under the Resource Efficiency dimension, that a complete picture can be formulated and effective decisions made.

In the diagnosis, facts, attitudes, and people's feelings are sought. Some of the areas included for investigation are: the adequacy of communications and information sharing; the suitability of problem solving, decision making, and planning; the ability of various departments to work together as a team and to fuse resources with others to accomplish objectives; and finally, the ability to achieve desired goals.

Within the context of these areas, the major categories that make up the MAP's Organization Effectiveness dimensions are:

- Extent and adequacy of *coordination,*
- Appropriateness and effectiveness of management,
- *Skills* and *orientation,*
- Adequacy of organization *structure,*
- Clarity of *goals* and goal-setting process,
- Composition and appropriateness of organization *climate.*

Extensive data are gathered and classified by subheadings of these categories (a total of over twenty) through a variety of instruments, individual interviews, and small-group meetings. The data are then analyzed to produce a rating in each major category for each department or functional unit. These ratings are combined with supporting conclusions and with a summary of those specific factors that are facilitating and those that are hindering the operation of the department.

4. How are Ratings Determined along Each Dimension?

RESOURCE EFFICIENCY DIMENSION

Basic questionnaires have been developed in each area to be mapped. Special tailoring is required to meet the needs of a particular organization. Members of the Mapping Task Force who are familiar with the particular functions being mapped complete the questionnaires in group sessions. A consultant also participates in the sessions. The questions are divided into basic categories:

a)   Questions that elicit *background information* and *basic characteristics*. They describe the inherent nature (complexity) of the problems faced. *No grading* is imposed on the answers to the questions.

   Examples
   • How many component and raw materials items are controlled?
   • What is the average number of levels per bill of material?

b)   Questions that request *measurement of performance*. A first step is for the Mapping Task Force to judge the weight of each dimension for the particular client. (For example, a toy manufacturer would have different weights of sophistication than would an aerospace concern.) Through individual and small-group meetings, points are assigned to each question in terms of the current status and the desired level of performance.

   The final score is a reflection of performance in areas with a high weighting, and it is these items that it is most important to highlight.

ORGANIZATION EFFECTIVENESS

COORDINATION

MANAGEMENT SKILLS AND ORIENTATION

GOALS AND DIRECTION

ORGANIZATION STRUCTURE

ORGANIZATION CLIMATE

ORGANIZATION EFFECTIVENESS DIMENSION

The organization effectiveness dimension covers the determination of the Organization Effectiveness rating, based on a systematic scoring of data gathered through:

• Individual interviews,
• Questionnaires administered to both individuals and small groups,
• Self-administered, validated data-gathering instruments.

Using these processes, information is gathered in five major categories and in over twenty subcategories for each function mapped.

Ratings in each subcategory are based on a scale of 1 (low) to 10 (high). Each subcategory is then weighted versus all others in the major categories, so that a weighted average rating can be determined for each major category. The rating for each function of the organization is determined from each of the category ratings. A total organization rating is then devised from the weighted ratings of each category for each department. A case study, Mapping Production Inventory and Purchasing Functions, is presented in the Appendix.

5.   How is the Mapping Effort Managed?

The consultants form a Mapping Project Management Team of client personnel during preliminary stages of a mapping project. The primary functions of this group are to:

a)   Offer administrative direction, establish interview dates, coordinate meetings, etc.
b)   Take part in making decisions regarding project direction, and
c)   Gather information from reports and other written documents needed to develop the MAPS.

This team has two major purposes.

*   The first is to *assure the client management* of the project.

    It is critical that the client have constant, up-to-date information on something as important as mapping. Through the Mapping Project Management Team, clients are able to make, or to participate in making, decisions regarding who should take part in the effort, how information concerning the project's progress should be dis-seminated, and how to sustain communication with top manage-ment on progress.

*   The second major purpose of the team is to *insure client participa-tion and involvement.*

    While this group may not be involved in conducting interviews, gathering information from small groups, or analyzing and drawing conclusions, its members do provide supporting data from their own impressions and from records, policy manuals, and reports. It is important that this input be considered and combined with that gathered by those doing the mapping.

6.   How Long does Mapping Take?

The answer to this question depends upon the scope of the project that top management selects, the size of the organization, the complexity of its management and/or production processes, the number of people to be involved, and the number of departments or functions that are to be mapped.

The cost per MAP tends to decrease substantially as the total number of MAPs to be made increases. Some managements may decide first to rank those resource areas believed to offer the greatest potential improvement, and then to concentrate on the top three or four. Other managements may want to have all resource areas included, particularly as the Organization Effectiveness dimension is probably less predictable. To offer a broad idea of scope, recently a small department with under ten people took part in a mapping effort. There was an average level of complexity (i.e., sequence planned, data gathered along both dimensions, and data analyzed). A MAP and factors that facilitated and hindered goal achievement were fed back.

The areas of greatest opportunity were presented in graphic form (see Fig. 3.3) that showed the key items for achieving most of the improvement. The total elapsed time period was three weeks. This example probably represents the least amount of elapsed time possible for a mapping effort.

C. ORGANIZATION

In recent industrial programs, we have achieved considerable success in reaching understanding and in gaining implementation support by combining the technical material with a small-group training approach. This method brings each individual's style and attitudes out into the open, where the group can deal with them in establishing the detailed objectives of the program. A key to success is that small groups are supportive of change and make it easier for individual exposure in carrying out the changes required. Such groups must include, at least, the task force and the functional managers who are directly involved in the program.

In one specific assignment, we worked with a steering committee composed of department managers who had authority for policy information. They were presented with basic data from our previous experience and other sources. Our Organization and Management Dynamics (OMD) staff helped them both in problem diagnosis and in improving the group's effectiveness in working together. The steering committee then created a Task Force to do the day-to-day work in the problem area—in this case Spare Parts Service—the most important profit item. The analysis and recommendations were presented to the Task Force, which had also been helped in diagnosis and effective communication by our OMD specialists. Our systems men worked with their counterparts on the Task Force. The Task Force developed a rapport with the steering committee through combined meetings and coordination by a few individuals who were members of both groups. Thus *policy* and *systems requirements* were blended together to achieve the desired systems designs. Furthermore, there was a high level of involvement on the part of all users

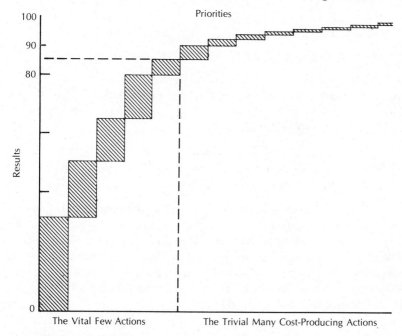

3.3 Chart of priorities

through this participation, producing a firm commitment to implement successfully to meet the agreed upon objectives.* The interpersonal and managerial factors causing delays were removed, and we were able to progress at a much faster rate.

The role of the steering committee and the Task Forces and their relationships to each other should be clearly understood. The steering committee should include all of the functional executives who have significant relationships to the MIS program. The chief executive or his designated senior officer should head the committee. In the policy and program formulation stages, the committee should be meeting several hours each week, while less frequent meetings can be held during the systems development phase. If the steering committee becomes a group without a mission, the program will fall short of objectives. Functional executives on the steering committee have to be dedicated to the MIS mission and insist on positive support within their own function. The Task Force leader and MIS head should be on the steering committee, as well as on the Task Force.

---

*"A New Look at the Functions of Managing People," *Personnel Administration* March–April 1965, by LeRoy G. Malouf, Jane S. Mouton, Robert R. Blake, p. 3. "A solution to the problem is achieved when each person not only takes responsibility for himself but shares responsibility for helping others to integrate their effort into an organized whole."

D. KEY FACTORS

1. Knowledgeable Support of the Chief Operating Executive

Nothing can replace the direct involvement of the chief operating executive, particularly in finding out whether the coordination he insists upon at the top is getting through to the bottom. People up and down the line read much into such executive interest:

> "The project must be important."
> "If it is not going correctly, the man who can change it knows."
> "It's all right to change methods even at the risk of some mistakes."

While the chief executive can observe the obvious, such as a void or confusion in communications, he cannot discover and analyze all of the problems that may arise. To do so, he needs an assistant with an objective view of the program (whether it be an outside consultant, an inside consultant, or a staff person), someone he trusts but who is not in charge. This is more demanding than the typical inspection role, because the person has to judge methods and performance more than results. Waiting to evaluate results may be too late in a complex, integrated management-information system. This person, with the Task Force leader and the chief operating executive, has to deal with the more serious emotional, political, and maturity problems that arise.

Lack of management interest is not the sole problem. There are instances in which management participation is high but inconsistent and diversionary. One company had excess inventories, poor schedule performance, and was operating at a loss. The survey indicated that the company had $1.8 million, or nearly 30 percent of its inventory, in inactive materials, because of a prior inept attempt to use Economic Ordering Quantities without update provisions. That company had three partially overlapping systems, the combination of which was still inadequate for control. A computerized requirements-planning system had been developed, but the stock record and allocation system still remained on accounting posting machines. A forward-planning system maintained due dates on all open orders, but almost universally these were overridden by an early stock-picking system that generated its own shortages. Many opportunities for economic grouping of setup had been missed. The duplicate-order control system was expensive, and the early pickups often confused the shortage picture when the schedule was changed.

Management wholeheartedly accepted the program to correct the situation by completing the conversion to a single computer-based system. The day the program started, the division manager resigned, because he felt the situation was not correctable within the time higher management allowed. Each successive manager promised to achieve successful operation within three months, only to be replaced when he failed to do so. Meanwhile, the chief executive actually supported programs that competed with MIS. In spite of these numerous changes and the related uncertainties, most of the program was ultimately accomplished when the last manager brought stability to the operation. However, much delay and extra costs were incurred along the way, not from lack of interest, but because of inconsistent program support and conflicts artificially created by the Chief Executive.

2. Competent Task Force Leader

One of the prime factors in a successful MIS program is the selection of the right Task Force leader. There is no single source of good candidates. Generally, extensive knowledge of the business functions is preferable to knowledge of systems or of a single product. All functional areas are important, and it is best to have a candidate with a background in three or more areas.

Obviously, background is not the only important requirement; leadership ability is essential. The demands and conflicts in user groups create substantial pressure, because of the amount of change associated with the program. There also is an important leadership demand within the group, especially in an eager young group that has less experience than is desirable.

The ability to communicate is a major requirement. The high communication demand is three-directional: up, sideways, and down. A poor job will not become good merely as a result of excellent communications, but a good job is often made ineffective by the lack of such communications. While most successful Task Force managers have different individual characteristics, there is a pattern to what they do well in the leadership role:

a. *Confidence*

They create an attitude of confidence within the task force and among most members of operating management. The task force confidence includes the capacity to listen, backed by the desire to make decisions and to bring all problems to the surface. There is a respect for, and a desire to be part of, the team. Operating management senses the situation and is also conscious of the communications coming in its direction.

b. *Professional Respect*

MIS is still a new world, one in which people work for and on programs they enjoy, rather than for pure financial advancement. The successful manager is technically competent, a good student in his own right, and he encourages his subordinates.

c. Service Orientation

The best managers want to see line and staff functions involved with and using the MIS system. In one company, a thoroughly competent MIS manager sought outside help on this matter and learned that, as he feared, he wasn't getting across to operating management on his own. The outsiders provided the catalyst in improving communications and bringing the two groups together.

The development and introduction of MIS have many characteristics that parallel a company's engineering and marketing functions to develop a complex new product. In both cases there must be plans, model development, tests, redesign, and sales. Master planning schedules have to be made and maintained.

In product development, the manager has to be concerned that the product is usable, will not require basic redesign too soon, is flexible, and can be adapted to meet new needs. It is surprising how many managers who have directed the successful development of new products have failed integrated business systems, while others have recognized the similarity right away and:

1. Made sure that line and staff managers wanted the features of the integrated system.
2. Insisted on an integrated design that avoided costly duplication of activities.
3. Developed a phased plan showing the resources required.
4. Estimated installation costs and forecasted return on investment.
5. Estimated the operating costs and savings of the new system by phases.
6. Presented the written plan, report, and PERT schedule so that the approved plan provided a freedom of action for the Task Force to work effectively.

3. Acceptable Rate of Change

The rate of change that is best for any company is highly variable. What appears slow to one company could be disastrously fast in another. The first word of caution is "Don't exceed your own best rate of change" to be followed quickly by "if your current best rate is too slow—do something about it." When a company exceeds its own acceptable rate, personnel become panicky, confidence is reduced, and time is spent on discussing the situation rather than getting the job done. The end result is not only slower completion but poorer quality as well.

What improves the acceptable rate of change? A management climate in which:

a) People are not blamed for initial mistakes in a new environment.
b) People are rewarded and praised if changes are successfully implemented rapidly and if they are involved in the process.
c) People associated with change are more likely to be promoted.
d) Changes are explained ahead of time at all levels.
e) People creating roadblocks to change are discovered and transferred if they don't react positively.

4. Organization and Management Development (OMD) Workshops

Having established one or more Task Forces with representatives from all of the functions and departments involved in the Management Information System, the OMD leaders proceed toward the development of an effective working relationship. Some of the people may not have established significant relationships with most of the others on the Task Force, while others may already have had continual involvement with one another—this involvement may have been cooperative or antagonistic, or somewhere between.

a) *A group develops better working relationships trying to solve unrelated problems.*

We can all easily be objective about other persons' problems—so starting here is advantageous for everyone. Role-playing can be part of some of the exercises. This gives the participants a chance to think of a problem from a different viewpoint. At times role reversal is helpful, and the manager becomes the worker; the Personnel Director becomes the Union Agent; etc.

b) *Prework on the problem both improves efficiency and indicates individual biases and style.*

Subgroups, or teams, of four to seven people may give individuals a better chance to express themselves and to improve working relationships.

c) *Subgroups and the larger Task Force develop skills in team operation.*

Some of the highlights of a team session are:

- Organizing the team and determining its relationship with top management.
- Selecting a chairperson.
- Setting objectives.
- Establishing agenda.
- Estimating timing.
- Discussing.
- Drawing conclusions.
- Critiquing the meeting.

While the group is working on many problems, an opportunity exists to demonstrate that the group working together achieves a result superior to any achieved by an individual in the prework; and, in such cases, the individual can see how his style, biases, or analysis led him to a solution that was less than the best. In cases where several teams are working on the same problem, a comparison of the teams' solutions may result.

Critiquing each meeting and comparing problem results to prior records helps each team evaluate its progress in working together and in reaching higher effectiveness levels.

Usually two three-day segments are required for the workshop, using actual or typical problems. Frequently the problems are within a framework similar to the type of problems the group will be trying to resolve later.

d)   *In the last portion of the workshop (perhaps another three days), one*
      or more of the company's MIS problems are presented to the group.
Usually these problems have been selected and worked up as case studies by the consultant and the members of the Task Force. Some examples of problems are:

- What are the priorities and sequence of computer systems applications?

- How do we get enough support from functions that may have to contribute more effort than they see returned in benefits (like Engineering improvement of bills of materials)?

- How do we get system integration when users are primarily concerned with their individual output?

As the teams receive the internal problems, usually a good carryover from the preceding group work is noticeable. Not infrequently a remark such as "That is not the way you acted two days ago, when you had my job in the case problem," is heard.

It is obvious that the first workshop is only a prelude to frequent meetings during these phases of an MIS system:

- Design,
- Development,
- Implementation, and
- Living with the system.

For these followup meetings, further technical prework is necessary. The OMD consultants observe progress intermittently. To regain perception, the groups should occasionally return to practice resolution of problems in workshop fashion. (Figure 3.4 tracks these steps diagramatically from onset to followup.)

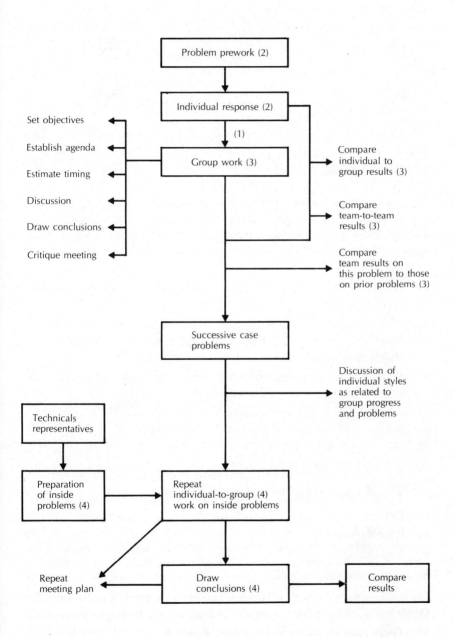

Figure 3.4

5. Task Force Separation From Current Operations

The task force concept has become accepted widely as one of the best ways to design and implement a multifunctional system. While some line representatives may not be required full time, the systems and programming members should be full-time.

The EDP manager may try both to run concurrent operations and to be the Task Force leader of major new systems applications. If he does this, either current operations or the new systems program will suffer, and sometimes both. If he is going to continue his responsibility for current operations, it is far better that he relinquish task-force leadership, be satisfied with part-time participation on the task force, and appoint a full-time representative.

In one MIS program, three task forces were created to develop parallel subsystems in marketing, manufacturing, and engineering under the guidance of a steering committee. The marketing and engineering task forces, over a three-year period, designed and implemented subsystems for:

● Forecasting

● Order entry

● Sales analysis

● Engineering project control

● Bill of materials

● Engineering change control

The manufacturing task force discovered at an early stage that significant inventory reductions were possible. They made appropriate recommendations for an interim program to reduce the inventory. They were then assigned to implement those recommendations. At the end of three years, they had not designed or implemented a single manufacturing system.

In a one billion-dollar corporation, the creation of several task forces, one for each division and one for each major corporate system, substantially improved effectiveness and the rate of progress. The systems manager and data-processing manager, who had been bottlenecks in the chain of command before, became ex *officio* members of all task forces. Their guidance became more acceptable than it had been before, in large part because they were no longer part-time leaders with full-time operating responsibilities.

6.   Encourage Cooperation between Functions

While the prime responsibility for creating a cooperative environment rests with the chief operating executive, individual functional managers can and must take positive, supportive action. They must:

- Be sure to appoint knowledgeable, competent people to the task force, preferably persons most likely to succeed the current managers.
- Be sure there is adequate knowledge of and attendance at coordination meetings designed to assure proper information flow.
- Give representatives maximum freedom of action without delegating final approval on major matters.
- Show department personnel support of MIS by regular reviews with their participation.
- Be willing to take responsibility to resolve conflicts with other functions.
- Maintain open and frequent contact with all other departments and inform superiors if any departments do not give reciprocal cooperation.

E.　NEED FOR COMMUNICATION BY FUNCTIONAL MANAGERS

One of our earliest and most successful installations of a practical, total system was in a process industry. While in retrospect it appears to have been a relatively trouble-free job, this was not always the opinion of management at the time. In this case, there was a brilliant systems and data-processing manager who could not communicate well with line personnel. The EDP manager failed to establish the schedule for his own department; he tended to accept and underestimate what he wanted to do, while he resisted and overestimated what others wanted. The danger in poor communications, however, is more serious in the sophisticated new area of computer applications than in the well-trod field of manual systems. At one point, we learned that the MIS program would be delayed seriously by a failure of his group to perform. Why? Because the data-processing manager had agreed to transfer accounts payable from central headquarters to his computer operations 1,500 miles away. How long a delay? A month to complete the transfer. New estimate? One more month. Actual result? Two more months. It was uncanny how often the "quickies" that EDP wanted took from two to three times longer than their own estimates!

The operations vice president was beside himself—he thought we had let him down when, in fact, we hadn't even been consulted! Perhaps, without the blowup, the delay would have lasted even longer. The movement of accounts receivable and payable was a recommendation we had made in a former survey. It was a good step, and it did save money; it was just made at the wrong time. The data-processing manager agreed to it willingly because it increased the scope of his department, and he wanted to please the controller. His prestige would have lasted longer if he had built more slowly and securely.

This systems and data-processing manager was probably more competent than many of his counterparts in other companies, but his next *faux pas* led to his replacement. Behind schedule on other important programs, he brought about another near-catastrophe by the "improvement" of the exponential forecasting program without consulting line management. Again the operations vice president had anger in his voice. "Why are these forecasts incompatible with the last report?"

"Because they are better," was the weak reply.

"Don't you realize that we have just had a two-day session explaining the new system to the whole sales force, and they need at least six months of continuity before we throw the changes at them—and even then the changes need to be thoroughly explained?"

"No."—just plain "no!" The EDP manager didn't think like that.

We have often marveled at this world of "anti-logic," where people take freedom and liberty when it is injurious but follow the letter of the law when practical judgment indicates that they should take liberty. It may be a natural immaturity carried over from adolescence to be exploring continually and subconsciously for boundaries. This is the only excuse for "anti-logic." But what a difference in final outcome when managers in both line and staff follow the rules they should and take practical liberties at the right time. This, more than almost any other trait, makes a competent manager in any field.

F.   EXCELLENCE VERSUS INADEQUACY OF IMPACT

There is no substitute for competent people. While we have emphasized this factor in our discussion of the Task Force leader, the same principle holds true for the supporting staff. A good manager knows his personnel and assigns work and applies controls in a way that produces the greatest effectiveness from the group. He has a wide range of capabilities to deal with. These people can be grouped into the categories described below.

1.   The Brilliant Overdesigners

People in this group usually have very high test scores but may produce less than their potential, because they make so many attempts to get that last 1 to 5 percent of computer efficiency. It is difficult to control this group effectively because its output still may be superior to the average programmer's, although nowhere near the potential output. It is important to have *frequent* discussions with these people to give approval to small segments of the project and seal off what already has been programmed *before* reaching the last 1 to 5 percent.

2. The Excellent Objective Type

These people aren't as challenged by the technical excellence of a particular phase but, by the interrelationships of a complex network, are thrilled to help build it. They contribute greatly when assigned broader responsibility with routine programmers working for them.

3. The Good Technicians

These people perform effectively if assigned tasks that are modest in scope, with reasonably clear boundaries. Broader or more complex work confuses them. They should *not* have supervisory responsibilities.

4. The Plodders

This group is enamored of the idea of programming, and loves to plunge into detail, but is excessively meticulous. For this reason, they produce only a fraction of the work of the others.

In the above analysis, we have not differentiated between systems people and programmers. Many companies insist that the same person do systems and programming work, and believe that only the level of skill is significant. There is an equally large group that insists the two be done separately. Our experience indicates that each approach has its place, depending on both people and situations. If a generalization had to be made, we would encourage systems analysts to program complex problems and delegate the programming in less complex areas.

G. ANALYSIS AND ACTION UPON PERSONNEL PROBLEMS

1. A sample of the facts involved and the work performed can point out the mentally lazy. A well-trained specialist can pin down superficiality in any systems area in a few days and within the whole operation in a not much longer period. The questionable leaders should be given one reprieve with full knowledge that the random sampling will be made again. A serious repetition of carelessness should result in transfer.

2. If insecure managers cause repeated delays, even though they have been encouraged continually to participate in "change," they should have their areas of responsibility reduced to the scope with which they can cope. People ultimately get more security and satisfaction from receiving praise on a smaller job than criticism on a larger one.

3. The task-force leader should encourage "top of the table" participation from all functions. People should be encouraged to admit small mistakes before the mistakes become big ones. Behind-the-scenes destructive comments or actions should be called out individually, and repeated actions should result in reassignment.

4. The egocentric quickly identifies himself, and there are many in this field. If he is not disruptive, it may be productive to give him staff assignments on specific projects, though frequently his approach is not practical because he cannot communicate with others. If the person is disruptive, transfer or termination is the only satisfactory answer.

5. We have observed several larger companies in which the political situation around systems development remains unresolved. Improvement creeps at a snail's pace. For this reason alone, we predict that the current lead held by middle-sized companies in computer-based information systems will increase rather than decrease. (This is contrary to the opinion of many experts that the larger companies lead in integrated information systems.) The major political problems can be dealt with only as the task-force leader and consultant identify them and secure the agreement of the chief executive.

H. SUMMARY

1. People must be given the confidence that it is "all right" to change habits and norms.

2. When people are given consideration and become involved themselves, their performance and cooperation improves even though some adverse conditions may thus be introduced.

In this chapter we have dealt with the all-important concern of management's attitude toward change as related to MIS implementation. Starting with the responsibilities of the chief executives, we outlined the organizational and operational problems that need resolution in most companies.

The creation and continuation of a positive attitude toward change is one of the major problems in installing integrated management-information systems. The problem is poorly understood and is usually resolved by inadequate action that comes too late. The fact is, however, that success in the computer age is as much related to the successful use and design of integrated business systems as to its acceptance by people who are expected to use it. There are important people problems in both design and use. These problems must be handled in a vastly improved manner in order to improve our effectiveness.

It is the top managers, not the specialists, who hold the key cards in this high-stakes game. And above all, the chief executive must be pragmatic about how much can be changed and how fast. In our opinion, top management usually adjusts fairly well to a dynamic environment. The greater difficulty lies in the proper preparation for the problems associated with "resistance to change" in the first place. This can be carried out by early involvement at several levels.

Involvement seems to be the key to dealing with this resistance, involvement on three levels. The first is with users of the system before it is designed. There should be a series of meetings between system designers and the people for whom the system is to be designed. It is here that MIS managers and analysts meet with first- and second-level managers from user organizations to gather data regarding the kind of information and service the user needs. The second level of involvement should come during system design and testing, when the MIS group has two responsibilities, (1) to develop a design that adequately responds to data gathered in the level above, and (2) to design and implement a training program to educate users in how to use the system. We will talk more about design in Chapter IV. The third level of involvement should take place after the system is designed and implemented and after the training sessions. It is here that the systems designers should maintain contact with users on a consulting basis, (1) assisting with problems and assisting users to more effectively use the system, and (2) adapting and changing the system to better respond to user needs.

QUESTIONS

1. *Testing the teams on the human side*

	Personal rating	Evaluation of the group
1. How will this affect me?		
2. Personally, will I be better off with the success or failure of the change?		
3. Shouldn't my greatest loyalty be to my own function?		
4. Shouldn't I get credit for all or part of a modified new proposal?		
5. Would my stature look better if that of the others looks worse?		
6. In this time of change, shouldn't I get a bigger job?		
7. Why should I do the extra work when the new and the old systems run in parallel?		
8. If I keep the old system accurately, won't the new look less attractive?		
9. If new information highlights problems that I know exist so that they become visible to my boss, will they blame me?		
10. Will I lose control in the conversion stage if problems arise that cannot be solved quickly?		

QUESTIONS—Continued

2. Mapping

How would you map the various functions in terms of systems effectiveness? On a scale from "1 = Poor" to "10 = Superior," assign values in column Y (Human Effectiveness) for each department. Then similarly assign values in column X (Technical Capability). Now plot the "ordered pairs" as single points, labeling by letters according to the following list:

a) Marketing
b) Engineering
c) Quality Control
d) Manufacturing
e) Material Control

f) Puchasing
g) Finance
h) Personnel
i) Distribution

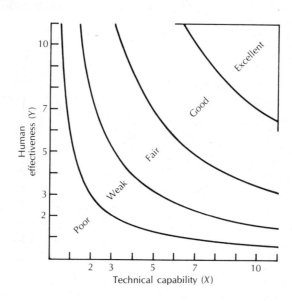

Figure 3.5

QUESTIONS—Continued

3. *How do you rate your Company on the following characteristics?*

	Poor	Slow	Average	Good	Excellent	Superior
Attitude toward the new system						
Adaptability to the rate of change contemplated						
Clarity of assignment to key Task Force leaders						
Adequate staffing in quality and quantity of the Task Force						
Commitment of key functional managers						

4. *Are we willing to talk with outside experts if we are uncomfortable with a significant number of these answers?*

4
Designing the System

A. MAJOR FACTORS

Four items of major significance have emerged in recent years as critical to the successful development of computer information systems:

a) The tremendous need for a Master Plan of implementation, spelling out resources (personnel and materials) and timetables.
b) The importance of "data base files" in eliminating both file and program duplication and proliferation.
c) The importance of the Task Force in integrating the organization and resolving different disciplines.
d) The necessity of data auditing and data improvement.

1.   Development, Approval, and Follow-up of a Master Plan

Another myth is that each subsystem within MIS can be dealt with independently and in a random sequence of application. At best such an approach builds substantial redundancy into the system, but in many cases, separate applications may waste time and money. For example, a good production-control system, developed independently, might schedule jobs tightly, but do so between an unknown *best start* date and an inaccurate *required finish* date. This hardly justifies an increase in computer cost to run the system. While there may be a number of ways to go, all effective installations must have a plan that involves a practical use of portions of the system as it develops, along with anticipated and future developments that progressively broaden the scope and use of the entire system.

a) Evaluation of the profit and performance-improvement potential generated by MIS in all functions and divisions.

It is surprising that so few managements have a Master Plan for Management Information Systems installation. But beyond this, many of the plans that exist are less than adequate. Plans for subsystems or equipment feasibility studies should not be confused with a complete Master Plan for the overall business system. Such plans may tabulate the requirements of the several functions and develop estimates of systems design, programming, and implementation time and costs, but still not consider the requirements for systems integration or common-data base organization. In one company without an integrated Master Plan, separate data-processing groups were supporting divisional headquarters, the engineering laboratories, and two manufacturing plants, with too large a staff in each location. Some of the staff in each place was required to interface with the partially duplicated system demanded by the other, and vice versa. The results were high costs and little progress. While this is an extreme example, the cases where plans have not dealt with systems integration or common data-base files are too numerous to recount. Effective Master Plans that lead to an efficient development program must include:

b)　Development of integrated MACRO systems diagrams and statements for the major systems, with preliminary approval from major functional heads.

Some companies never develop a MACRO system design. This causes substantial difficulties and increases operating costs. Many of those who do prepare a MACRO system do not have the benefits of a cost-and-benefits schedule to help them. Thus, these people are limited to designing a system that conceptually meets operating requirements but may not be practical and does not aim directly at areas where potential savings exist.

There are many factors which influence the MACRO design. Most of these factors are facets of the nature of the business.

Marketing—What type of product do we sell?

Standard products	Seasonal
Standard plus specials	Repair or spare parts
Special products	

Distribution—How do we sell and distribute the product?

Ship direct	Operate single or
Ship to warehouses	Multilevel warehouse
Ship to retailers	Combination of the above

Engineering and Product Structure—How complex is the product (and the data base necessary to describe it)?

Single-level structure	Special engineering
Multilevel structure	requirements

Manufacturing—How do we actually make it?

Process	Common versus unique parts and assemblies
Mass production	Planned and/or unplanned demand
Bench assembly	Alternate operations
Job-shop/foundry	Work standards and workloads

Purchasing—How do we obtain outside materials?

Blanket orders	Vendors' performance,
Price breaks	price, quality, time
Make or buy policy	
Vendors	

Accounting—How do we measure performance?

Standard cost and variance	Job costs
Direct cost and marginal income	Pricing

It is seldom difficult to develop a superficial description of a company:
We sell a standard product with options direct to the customer. The product is complex, with mutilevel product structure, manufactured and assembled in small lots with some purchased parts. We use a standard cost system.

This description may be adequate for some purposes, but it is only a starting point for the MACRO system designer. It gives him a clue to some of the questions he must ask:

- How "standard" is the product?
- How extensive and/or special are the options?
- Are the options added at the end or built in during the process?
- Do they require special engineering design?
- Do bills of materials adequately describe the product—
    for engineering? for manufacturing? for accounting?

One of the major outputs of the MACRO design is a closer approximation of the size of the task that lies ahead in implementing MIS. The MACRO design is still basically conceptual but it is one step closer to the real world. With a more precise description of the nature of the company and what might best be called the "management requirements" of MIS, the MACRO system designer is ready to explore how it might be done. His starting point is the *data base.*

While the total requirements are not known at this point, the MACRO design should include the development and approximate assignment of all known data fields to integrated records in data-base files and the assignment of input responsibility. It is important that the assignment of responsibility for data fields and for the timeliness and accuracy of data input be made as early as possible. Failure to do this can lead to a confusion and delays in data preparation and data input, as well as inadequate error control later. Recent experience indicates that data cleanup must start at the inception of the MIS program, so that good data can be ready by the time of implementation. We have seen numerous instances where the system was ready to go, but the data base had not been cleaned up yet. Finally, the MACRO design should include the following:

1. Listing of all major and some minor programs that will be required to support each major area, with sequence and timing of the major milestones.
2. Estimation of manpower and timing requirements and sequence of application of the program.
3. Estimation of equipment requirements in a plan that is compatible with the growth of the system.
4. Recommendation of task force(s), responsibility assignments, coordinating groups, and so on.

When a study has been completed covering these major points, and a report submitted, approved, and supported by top management, then a company has a complete Master Plan that has a high potential of succeeding. The people assigned to MIS can now work more effectively, with minimum political interference, toward the common goals that have been established.

2. Early Start of Policy Determination Related to MIS

Unfortunately, many managements fail to realize that there are significant policy determinations or revisions related to MIS. We have observed a high correlation between excessive design and programming costs, and lack of policy determination. This is one of the key points in MIS development: Clarification of policies is desirable in itself, as well as producing beneficial results when policy interpretations are carried out through the MIS system. A system without policies ends up as either an automated data manipulator, which is largely ignored, or a system that is severely criticized because managers using it make decisions and produce results that are inconsistent or not in accordance with corporate objectives.

Some of the policy areas requiring management decision are contained in the following outline:

I. Overall Policies

Executive approval
 of MIS Master Plan
Task Force responsibilities
Systems development
Cost of money, price
 breaks, EOQ limits

Product lead-time delivery
 or service rate
Quantity discount on product-
 pricing strategy
Responsibility for master
 scheduling

II. Sales and Marketing

Pricing	Service
Warranty	Agents
Spares	

III. Engineering

Numbering	Bills of material
Tolerancing	Engineering change control
Specials versus standard	Configuration management

IV. Manufacturing—Industrial Engineering

Routing	Labor control
Operation sheet	Work centers
Standards	

V. Material—Production and Inventory Purchasing Control

Material requirments planning (MRP)	Contract ordering
	Price-break limits
EOQ rules, limits	Split lots
Safety stock	

VI. Distribution

Holding areas	Direct shipment
Partials	Drop-off
Contracts	

VII. Financial—Accounting

Separate versus integrated cost system	Job costs
	Closing inventory valuation
Standard cost-variance	Obsolescence
Direct costs	

3. Common Data Base for All Multipurpose Information

Another myth is "Keep EDP applications simple." While no one can defend unwarranted complexity in information and control systems, the truth is that many of the operations being controlled are, in and of themselves, very complex. Furthermore, the more complex they are, the more likely it will be that the computer application will pay big dividends. It is tempting, but utopian, to pursue the idea that "There is a simple solution to this problem if only we are smart enough to find it."

One general manager, with a complex problem relating to a bill-of-material time-phased explosion of requirements, responded to the "keep it simple" suggestion by withdrawing his support of the new computer system, and attempted to solve the problem with a simple punched-card system. He had found that he could not get sufficient payback with merely a faster data-recording system, and eventually the program went ahead as originally planned. A strong interest in improved operations and payback is typical of companies that report a real improvement and significant benefits from computerization.

One of the more difficult, but important, tasks is the development of common data bases for multipurpose information. The task is difficult because the requirement for such action comes so early in the whole program and because interfunctional agreement and dependency are required. Frequently, accounting, which does not need the detail on labor reporting desired by production control and inspection, may request that its program be applied earlier with less time and cost. This is one of the first instances of the development of independent programs for a functional area with an unavoidable cost of redoing when the systems for the other functions are later unified. Similar instances can also occur in sales, engineering, and manufacturing, even though they should use the common data base more than should accounting.

The data-base concept carries with it a coordination requirement between functions, as to what and where data will be stored. The responsibility to maintain the data accurately and on schedule is also fundamental. Such action affords the system designers a firm foundation upon which to build. Our experience indicates that substantial time losses have occurred in the past because of the uncertainty of the data source; and, in some cases, redundancy has been accepted in order to proceed.

There is a general agreement on the minimum number of main files needed for MIS. These are described below. There is no agreement on the maximum number because in many cases costs and performance can be improved by splitting the main files. This does not imply redundant fields between files, but is an attempt to balance the cost of readdressing the split files with a reduction in transfer time needed for reading a larger file.

Data-Base File Structure

Most integrated business systems can operate very satisfactorily with from 10 to 20 basic data files. In addition to these, there may be working files that support various subsystems. These files are likely to be data in transition, or data generated for a unique end purpose, as contrasted to the "always available for everybody" nature of the basic data files.

The basic data files can be logically grouped around the major functional area to which they give prime support, but they also can be used by other subsystems when needed.

Table 4.1 Classification of files.

Files	Fields	Comments
Systems Area: Order entry and master planning		
1. Open customer orders (Accts. Receivable)	Sales order number High-Level numbers Prices Order dates Due dates Commission rate Customer order number Balance due	Accounts Receivable may be a split file.
2. Customer master file	Customer code Name and address Credit status ABC class SIC group Geo. code Billing instructions Shipping instructions Salesman code. Credit status Shipping instructions	
3. Finished inventory (Item master)	Part number Description Special codes Lot size Reorder point Assembly usage Spares usage Quantity on hand Quantity on order Lead time ABC code Product code Unit of measurement Engineering change status Safety stock Low-level code Source code Manufacturing grouping code Forecasting Alpha Shrinkage factor	Usually the same as lower level of component part record.

Files	Fields	Comments
Systems Area: Requirements planning and order generation		
3.—*continued*	Keys to other records	
	Usage history	May be split into
	Cost data	separate file.
	Activity code	
	Unit price	
	Discount codes	
4. Product structure	Parent part number	
	Component part number	
	Description	
	Engineering codes	
	Change status	
	Quantity per lot	
5. Item master		See Finished inventory file
6. Open purchase orders (Accts. Payable)	Purchase order number date	
	Part number	Accounts Payable may
	Description	be a separate file.
	Quantity ordered	
	Quantity released	
	Due date	
	Deliver to	
	Price	
	Vendor	
	Buyer number	
	Quantity received	
	Balance due	
	Overdue	
	Rejected quantity	
	Receiving report number	
7. Vendor master	Vendor number	
	Name	
	Address	
	SIC group	
	Geo. code	
	Payment information	
	Terms	
	History	
	Shipping instructions	
	Delivery rating	
	Quality rating	

Files	Fields	Comments
Systems Area: Order Generation		
8. Purchase master	Part number	
	Description	
	Vendor codes	
	Current quotes	
	Price breaks	
	Quality record	
	Delivery record	
	Last order	
Systems Area: Scheduling and Loading		
9. Payroll (Personnel)	Social Security number	
	Employee number	
	Name	
	Skill class	
	Prior skills	
	Employment date	
	Birth date	
	Assignment	
	Scrap record	
	Tardy record	
	Performance record	
	Wage rate	
	Cumulative pay	
	Cumulative taxes	
	Overtime	
	Deductions	
10. Open factory orders	Factory order number	
	Part number	
	Description	
	Engineering change status	
	Last activity date	
	Quantity	
	Due date	
	Routing—by operation number	
	Set-up hours	
	Cycle hours	
	Status codes	
	Labor to date	
	Scrap, variance	

Files	Fields	Comments
Systems Area: Scheduling and Loading (continued)		
11. Routings	Part number Operation number Work Center number Lead time Standard set-up hours Standard cycle hours Tooling Alternate operations	
12. Work-center master	Work center number Description Efficiency factor Man capacity Machine capacity Hours input Hours output Hours in queue	
Systems Area: Distribution		
13. Item master at branch	Part number Description On hand On order Back orders Reorder point Usage Forecast	Repeat of some of Item Master File
14. Network load (for each) (for each)	Branch Open order parts Forecast delivery Quantity Due date	
15. Customer history		Repeat some of customer information file
16. Operation sheet master		May be a part of routing
17. Tooling		May be a part of routing
18. Machine group		May be a part of work-center master

Working Files

REQUIREMENTS

A list of all demands on the company by part number at all levels chained to customer order, forecast order, or master schedule control, usually produced by an explosion using a bill-of-material processor.

REPLENISHMENTS

A list of manufacturing or purchase orders created where the stock on hand at all levels was inadequate to satisfy the requirements.

Working files, such as requirements and replenishments files, frequently are organized serially and may not be available to direct access; but they permit the regeneration of data in the master files at a far more rapid rate than would be possible by inserting data directly.

Another characteristic of working files is that the data may be current for only a short period of time and then be inactive. This is typical of shop orders, requisitions, and so on.

Data-base Files, however, give freedom rather than confinement to a systems group. Knowing the current and future availability of data and its exact location permits the systems designer to proceed more rapidly and with greater certainty toward usable programs.

The adoption of the data-base file concept places a high responsibility upon each function for the timeliness and accuracy of the data being submitted from its portion of the operations, because others are now directly dependent on high-quality performance, where, before, each function messed up its own operations.

4.   Management-by-Exception Reporting in Systems Design

How often is management by exception talked about, and how often is it used in system design? It is talked about continuously, and yet one of the most frequent complaints heard from computer users concerns "the mountains of reports" or "being snowed by the paper-output monster." It is also strange that where exception routines have been developed, they have not been used fully because of a lack of education and confidence.

It is unfortunate that not every major systems staff has a practical statistical analyst who could structure some of the controls that govern exception reports. It is not necessary to cover these controls here as they were adequately discussed in *Unified Operations Management in 1963,** but a listing will serve as a reminder.

a)   Use of ABC stratification for parts, products, customers, vendors, costs, and so on.

---

* *Unified Operations Management,* Putnam, Barlow, and Stilian. McGraw Hill, 1963.

b)   Use of control limits to indicate items out of control, particularly upon update of forecast, usage, costs, EOQ's, and so on.
c)   Use of coding to carry management intent into action.
d)   Use of a pyramid building-block structure in report design to present the desired amount of detail at the appropriate organizational level.

In some cases, systems designers have heard of these techniques, but they can't find anyone in the functional areas who has the time or knowledge to do the initial analysis. In other cases, the concepts are hazy to both groups. Sometimes, when such techniques are suggested by users, the systems group shies away because additional programming complexity will be required and the project is already behind schedule. We must conclude that the proponents of "management by exception" must become more hardnosed about this demand, or it will continue to be slighted in the future.

The cases where design has been adequate but usage of management-by-exception reports is low present a different problem. Managers have to be taught how to use "exception" reports to improve operations and to rely on computer accuracy and logistics for the routine decisions; then they will stop asking for the complete printouts, including those for B and C items. We need more A item managers.

5.   Development and Approval of User's Systems Specifications

In far too many programs, the desired results of the management information system are not specified carefully by the using departments. This leads to two serious conditions.

a)   The existing vagaries of current decision making are not defined clearly for the new system. Clearing up policies for business decisions would make the systems work in a more straightforward manner.
b)   The demands on the system development group are revised and increased as the users see expanded opportunity. This delays program development without identifying the responsibility for the delay and the extra cost.

The user specs should cover the detail and frequency of output both in specific and in summary form. The content of programs must be covered in terms of logic required. These specifications should be organized in both operational and functional categories:

Operational	*Functional*
Forecasting	Sales reports
Order entry	Statistics
Product structure	Shipping

Engineering change control	Engineering
Requirements	Product design
Replenishment	Production
Inventory control	Materials management
Scheduling	Production control
Ordering	Purchasing
Accounts payable	Accounting
Payroll	

Usually, the operations specifications can best be written by members of the task force who are oriented toward the integration requirements of the system, and then be approved by the functional managers concerned. The functional specifications should be written by the functional managers (or other representatives on the task force), but then be reviewed with the others for redundancy or inconsistency.

These specifications should also cover the frequency of service for both specific and generalized output. Even though these requirements may change in the future, the logistics of file structure, information retrieval, and processing methods will be influenced by this documentation. Frequently, the use of decision tables aids in the clarification of many gray areas that would be difficult to program accurately.

The internal specifications can best be shown by a combination of a flow diagram, systems input, transaction required, output sheet, and a verbal description of the formulas and methods involved. We have found that a page or more describing each transaction leads to both better modular control and clearer understanding between designer and user. The user representative should always sign these sheets.

While final specifications are difficult to write completely and accurately at the outset, the effort to do so should bring many things to light that could be more costly to deal with later. It is always easier to modify a plan that has been developed than to deal with a new request when specifications have not been prepared previously.

One of the best ways is to decide upon the logistical requirements during the Master Plan Survey. With this already completed, it should be possible, by discussion with line and staff management (using further simulation in complex situations), to establish parameters for design in customer service rate, forecasting, ordering, scheduling, and safety stocks. These may not be the detail specifications needed for programming, but they at least set the boundaries of the design. These specifications, which are really statements of company policy, are the hardest to finalize; but sometimes trouble is encountered in areas of output design, availability of data on inquiry, frequency of update, and the like.

6. Data Editing and Control

It is difficult to believe that there are systems in existence today that do not include comprehensive transaction editing; but there are, despite the fact that GIGO (Garbage In–Garbage Out) has been a popular and somewhat descriptive computer term for years. Conversely, some systems have been designed with such tight editing provisions that the volume of rejected transactions exceeds the capacity of people to correct them. One of the key elements in the final performance of MIS is both the completeness of editing all data entering the system and the resolution of errors that are detected. This may require a compromise between the EDP staff and the user, based on their evaluation of the impact of undetected and/or uncorrected errors. At a minimum, we feel that the design should incorporate these features:

a) There should be a format EDIT which rejects transactions if required data is missing or in the wrong format:

   Example: "Quantity issued is blank or not numeric."

b) There should be tests for illogical or undesirable conditions which may reject or issue warning messages but always highlight the condition.

   Examples

   1. An issue causes the on-hand balance to become negative.
   2. A cycle count results in an inventory loss greater than $1,000.
   3. Production reports making 120 pieces when the order quantity is 100.

The design must specify whether transactions will be conditionally accepted or rejected outright. In addition, a data-control procedure must be written to specify how all errors will be corrected. During implementation, training in data control will be extremely important.

7. Inadvisability of Poor Documentation or Other Shortcuts

The temptation to take shortcuts, particularly at times of crisis, must be guarded against. These actions are likely to develop at lower levels and frequently go unobserved by the managers who are interested in meeting observable deadlines and do not check on the quality of work that has been "completed." The pressure to meet deadlines sometimes leads to the employment of moonlighters for programming, which can cause further difficulty because it fails to achieve a quality job that is adequately documented. This does not apply to competent programming companies who contract for specific tasks and have a proven record of accomplishment.

The protection against these actions is an alert higher-management group that occasionally reviews in depth the competence and thoroughness of the programming and documentation work. Management has to be involved to find out about the adequacy of programming and, when it is, the results are good.

As a guide to what to expect of documentation during the early design stages, we have included below excerpts from Rath & Strong's Internal Documentation Manual developed in January, 1973.

B. SYSTEMS AND PROGRAMMING DOCUMENTATION

Systems and program documentation, as defined herein, is the combined product of systems designers, analysts, programmers, and procedure writers. The basic requirements are that client systems analysts and/or programmers with normal aptitude, experience, and motivation could take over and maintain the systems and/or programs without further support from Rath & Strong; and that user personnel will be able to process inputs and outputs effectively. Complete documentation, depending on the complexity of the system or program, may require any or all of the following:

- System proposal
- System description
- Program documentation
- Policies and procedures

1.0 System Proposals

The documentation process begins with the preparation of a proposal for work with a client. As part of the task definition in the proposal, the type and degree of documentation that will be provided should be clearly specified. It is recognized that the time that can be included in a proposal for documentation is frequently limited by cost constraints. Reduced time allowances will result in overrun or reduced quality and/or quantity in the final product.

2.0 Application Description

The Application Description is conceptually oriented; it describes the problem to be solved and the concepts, methodology, formulas, etc., which are used to solve the problem. The most comprehensive Application Description which Rath & Strong has prepared is the PIOS manual. Its table of contents is listed below with a brief description of each section.

2.1 Introduction

2.2 The Environment

The problem statement, or what the system is designed to do.

2.3 Inventory Control Concepts

Description of the techniques used in this module, e.g., requirements planning.

2.4 Production Control Concepts

Same for the Production Control module.

2.5 System Description

Brief description of how the system works. An overview of the next level of documentation. A more detailed System Description is a separate document, described in the next section.

2.6 Computer System Concepts

Description of some of the unique computer capabilities used in the system.

2.7 Implementation

What must be done to install the system, including time and cost.

2.8 Summary

Benefits provided by the system:
An Application Description is one of the outputs of a system survey. It serves several functions which are critical to the system development process:

- Statement of objectives
- Estimated costs and benefits
- Concepts appropriate for solving the client's problem
- Basis for client agreement to proceed with next phase of development

The Application Description can be considered a sales tool. It is directed toward the client decision maker and should provide him with justification (assuming it exists) for proceeding with the project. It provides only broad guidelines for those who will be responsible for subsequent implementation.

3.0 System Description

The System Description is implementation-oriented; it provides the implementation task force with a generalized knowledge of how the system is expected to work. When combined with the Application Description, it should provide the Task Force with sufficient information to proceed with detail system-development process. In many instances, the System Description is generated in the survey stage. If this is to be done, it should be clearly stated in the proposal, and separate time and cost estimates should be prepared.

The System Description should cover the following areas:

3.1 System Flow Chart

3.2 Program Descriptions

3.3 Input Transactions
a) Preliminary layouts
b) Basic logic

3.4 Output Reports
a) Preliminary layouts
b) Frequency and distribution

3.5 Data Base
a) Files required
    1. Key data elements identified
b) File management system

3.6 Computer Requirements
a) Hardware configuration
b) Software
c) Estimated processing time

3.7 Policy and Procedural Requirements
a) Management decisions
b) Training program

3.8 More Detailed Implementation Plan

4.0 Design Review and Approval

With the completion of the Application and System Description, it is possible to make a reasonably accurate estimate of the implementation schedule. Prior to this time, there are too many unknowns to permit commitment to a firm schedule.

4.1 Design Freeze

It is recognized that systems design is a dynamic process and that changes will occur through the implementation stage. However, the basic concept should be frozen at the time of Design Review and Approval, since a major change in direction could make all prior estimates invalid.

4.2 Realistic Schedule

The schedule should be based on expected workload and available resources, not on an arbitrary desired completion date.

4.3 Commitment of Resources

Key people should be assigned to the implementation task force in support of the schedule. Where appropriate, allowance should be made for startup delays, getting the people, and so forth.

C. INTERACTION BETWEEN FUNCTIONS AND CLARIFICATION OF DETAILS

Time and again we observe endless delay and misunderstandings because relatively minor details are not clarified between the functions involved. Under constructive leadership with a competent support staff, these problems can be handled so quickly and easily that they hardly seem to exist at all. The following examples show a variety of these interfunctional conflicts.

a)   The chief engineer and the manufacturing manager debate the use of the bill-of-material list in place of meaningless drawings on "cut to length only" items.

b)   The configuration management department and the manufacturing department struggle over redundancy in issue and control of thousands of standard specification drawings.

c)   A company task force rejects a proposed order-entry system and then proposes an almost identical proposal after nine months of "study."

d)   A purchasing accounts payable system is not integrated because one field needed by purchasing is not available.

e)   A distribution/plant inventory operation is not integrated because one unit-of-measure field is not agreed upon.

f)   A simplified engineering release system is in jeopardy because print lists will not be supplied for packages of drawings to be released to production.

g)   Two forecasting systems remain incompatible because one group wants statistics by months and quarters for one year, while the other group wants a six-month block.

These may seem subject to straightforward reconciliation, they are, but not if each department holds fast to its own desire to win. There is a range in attitudes from functions that want to cooperate fully to those that don't want any compromises at all. In between are those who avoid decisions and drag their feet when not observed. The participative workshops should help surface and resolve these types of issues.

D. ALLOWING FOR EXPANSION

Occasionally, we hear management complain of the restricted flexibility of a computer system. In one case, the very manager making the complaint was the same person who insisted that additional data would not be needed when it was suggested the year before. While we can criticize the manager, we should also point out that the systems designer should have included "filler" space (area reserved for future use) in the files for further growth. Computer systems can be extremely flexible in presenting a variety of reports from the same data and in changing the use of the data by logistical coding. However, if there is no filler space left in the record, then the cost of reorganizing the files can be very expensive. Usually 5 to 25 percent is adequate, depending upon the nature of the file. The product-structure file and routing file need little filler (because their content is fairly standardized) as compared to the master part record, inventory files, and those that generate statistics that may be coded in new ways and split into new areas.

E. OPERATING SYSTEMS, DATA BASE MANAGEMENT SYSTEMS, SOFTWARE

This section is not intended to be a treatise on software, which would require many volumes, nor is it intended for the EDP professional. It is intended to present some of the current computer jargon that is widely used in the MIS field.

1. Programming Languages

Management has the choice of programming languages that are highly machine-oriented or those that are highly machine-independent. The former operate the most efficiently but, being machine-dependent, require substantial reprogramming when a new generation of equipment is developed. The higher-level languages (such as COBOL or FORTRAN) require more core for the same programs and operate somewhat more slowly than the machine-oriented languages. The high-level languages are easily convertible to new hardware. The higher level languages provide easier documentation that is more readily understood by different personnel than do the machine oriented languages.

Here again, the needs of the situation may lead to the best answer. If a company enters on a five-year program to install an integrated management-information system, which may have one or more changes of hardware during, or shortly after, the installation, the ease of changing programs to keep pace is extremely important. If a company has completed its programs and the reprogramming time is a small percentage of the total time between computer generations, concern for computer efficiency is important and machine-language operation makes better sense.

2. Operating Systems

An operating system is a collection of programs, supplied by the computer manufacturer, which performs many common or repetitive functions within the computer, relieving the programmer of the need to code these operations in each of his programs. Each manufacturer offers several operating systems with a range of capabilities and sophistication. Of concern to general management are two aspects of operating systems that could have an impact on the MIS program.

a)   Every operating system has restrictions; none support *all* of the other software and data-base management systems that are available in the marketplace.

b)   Changing operating systems can be time-consuming and expensive, and could have an impact on the MIS schedule.

Generally speaking, however, operating systems decisions are made on purely technical grounds and should be delegated to the EDP Manager. Companies with small or medium-size computer needs should avoid full operating systems that have high core requirements for their own support.

3. File Organization and Maintenance

The organization of files in tape systems is restricted by what the specific tapes and the related programs involve. The third-generation disk systems, the addressing, relating, adding, and deleting of files is much more complex. Consequently, software now provides for the automatic indexing and relating of the records in the files.

To use this accurate and efficient software, the programmers have to follow the precise rules specified. One of the more complex programs is the Bill of Material Processor. This program creates complete interrelationships between the parts, subassemblies, and assemblies at all levels. The amount of time required to create such software is sufficiently large to make it practicable in all but the largest companies. The latter group may find it worthwhile to develop specific software of this type for themselves.

4. Data-Base Management Systems (DBMS)

A DBMS is a collection of programs that permits the efficient organization, maintenance, and retrieval of multiple files. A DBMS increases both programmer and computer efficiency, and reduces data redundancy in the various files. The earliest and most widely used DBMS is IBM's Bill-of-Material Processor (BOMP), which integrates:

- Part-number master file
- Product-structure file
- Work-center master file
- Standard routing file

In recent years a number of other systems have become available at widely varying prices. These systems permit retrieval of fields or record segments other than the complete record. If you plan to use one of the later systems, you would be wise to perform a cost/performance study before making the final decision.

5. Application Software*

In the last three years, there has been considerable growth in applications software. In spite of the areas of greatest need, the accounting application practices dominate in sales volume at the present time.

Application packages have certain advantages that are particularly attractive in the MIS field; for example:

a) *Cost*. Packages normally sell for 10 to 15 percent of the development cost.
b) *Speed*. Significant reductions in detail design, programming, and system testing time are possible.
c) *Reliability*. Unless you are the "guinea pig," the package has been fully tested and debugged elsewhere (you can and should verify this).

Against these advantages, you have to consider the possibility that available packages:

a) Do not fit your requirements;
b) Need modification that significantly increase the time and expense to install; or
c) Do not include guaranteed support in the event that something does go wrong.

Our projection is for forecasting, production, and inventory control, MRP and distribution to pick up support gradually. Eventually, this will become the greatest area of systems sales because of both the complexity and the volume.

6. System Sensitivity Directed toward Real Needs

In the first application of critical-ratio scheduling it became apparent that daily adjustment in priorities was necessary to reduce expediting and overtime costs. This was a far greater sensitivity than the inventory-control system (designed a year before) would permit. What irony! The use of a significant new development in scheduling was restricted by a so-recently implemented inventory-control system. Moreover, those orders that were predominantly for parts to be used in sub- or final assembly had some inaccuracies in the calculation of priority. If the assembly schedule were modified, the replenishment order coming

---

*A more thorough discussion of manufacturing Software Packages is presented in Appendix 3.

through the manufacturing or purchasing department might not be adjusted accurately. Thus, in some of these cases, the expediter following back the real needs from the assembly floor had superior information than that in the computer-based system. Secondly, the critical-ratio calculation for stock replenishment was affected by the degree to which the requirements for a particular assembly order were reserved. If the items were reserved for assembly too early, the critical ratio would expedite the replenishing order because there was less available stock. Such action was likely to tighten up the ratio too soon, in comparison to those orders that were coming through manufacturing without such a reservation having taken place. A system can be either oversensitive or not sensitive enough. The sensitivity should meet needs and be properly balanced between order due dating and expediting. If expediting is done to the closest week on the assembly schedule, then the computer programs must deal with weekly demands, and must provide for weekly scheduling and preferably daily posting, if they are going to be sufficiently current to replace manual expediting. If the stock on hand were large enough to satisfy the subassembly or assembly requirements for a stated period of time, the expedite ratio could bring in the replenishment order while the assembly floor's requirements had already been covered by the last issue.

Critical ratio's use for spare parts items ran satisfactorily. It is important that good due dates be set and maintained by MRP systems in "dependent demand" situations. If, on the other hand, we deferred the reservation of the assembly items until almost the point of actual use on the assembly floor, the critical ratio on the part coming through would be too slack. Then there might not be enough lead time left in which to close the order when needed. Furthermore, the magnitude of the demands in any biweekly or monthly period would be so large that when the reservation was made it would drastically affect the ratios in the schedule. As a compromise, a single-time system was retained for reservations—but with backdating by component lead time to adjust priority. Thus, the total reservations helped trigger orders related to reorder points, but, in determining schedule position (i.e., how far into the future the on-hand balance provided coverage), the available stock compared with progress in the plant was used. This was not as good as the real time-phased critical-ratio systems to be developed later (because it did not permit readjustment of due dates once the order was released against its own lead time), but it was a start.

Where a business has to respond to demands recognizing time differences in the required actions, no simplification of single-time system will meet the needs, and much of the computer system's effort will be limited if this approach is ignored. A time-phased system shows the exact point in the future when the available stock would be insufficient to cover reservations. This would give the best schedule date for the receipt of the replenishment order.

We see evidence, wherever this principle is overlooked, that foreman's clerks and expediters hang on and can justify their existence by running a more realistic system than does the computer-based program.

Another area of sensitivity is that related to realistic needs on the assembly floor. Many industrial products require from one to five months for assembly, but little effort is made to phase the production order to the time of real need at assembly. Overtime is wasted and inventories are unduly high when all parts are scheduled to arrive at the beginning of the assembly period, despite the fact that many will not be needed for weeks or months.

7.   Modular Design

In second-generation systems, little thought was given to modular design. Many programs were developed under the concept, "if the record has been transferred into computer, do the maximum amount of processing with it." While this made sense at the time, such philosophy does not fit as well into third-generation systems. Increased core capacity and data-base systems permit a program today to perform far more complex functions. Thus, the choice of doing everything possible to one record, versus updating all of the data base for a given function in modular steps, becomes more favorable to the latter. There are several reasons:

a)   Programs that are not modular are difficult to improve in part and may require complete reprogramming.
b)   Programs that are not modular may require complete processing daily, while modular programs permit different frequencies and partial updating.
c)   Modular programs are easier to transfer from one installation to another (i.e., between divisions and plants).
d)   Modular programs are easier to debug.

The subsystem design along modular lines requires more careful planning by the Task Force leader and the senior systems analysts. Though more time is required in early stages, this is more than offset by increased flexibility later, which permits more efficient assignment of programmers.

Modular programs appear to offer an easier and more flexible base for conversion for each successive generation of computers. This may turn out to be the most significant advantage of all.

8.   Danger of Overemphasis on OR Theory

In general, we favor the integration of an operation-research approach in an implementation program. In one circumstance, however, the delays in preparing for the installation indicated that the manual implementation of simplified operations research-type rules could bring benefits even if applied ahead of the computer system. Another company implemented economic-lot ordering, time scheduling, and warehouse inventory rules, and made substantial inventory and scheduling savings for a significant period before the new system was installed. Sometimes there has been an underlying feeling that a corporate systems group can only improve the systems application and will not have an actual impact on the division profitability. This attitude limits the effectiveness of corporate operations-research personnel.

It is difficult to give an operations-research group sufficient practical experience to bridge the gap between the line requirements and the theoretical models. In many instances, it is almost as if the OR group were on the staff of some remote university and attempting to solve a problem that had been presented by complete strangers.

This results in little application of operations-research work. In one case, an operations-research department of ten men accomplished little of practical value in a period of several years; yet the company had many areas of potential improvement that could have resulted from the use of the simplest decision rules. The difficult problem for operations-research personnel is in understanding the practical situation, the numerous restrictions, and the fitting of the solution into the environment. When this is accomplished, the line people must reach an understanding of the solution to the problem so they can work with operations-research, rather than subvert or unintentionally abort it. There is an apparent reluctance on the part of young, technically trained personnel to become involved in production and to become acquainted with the real world. This is unfortunate, because probably the largest single area of payback for the use of the computer in the industrial world lies in the complex manufacturing scheduling-control applications, which require the practical understanding and the approach of a realist who can bring about a solution with the support of the computer.

9.   Importance of Quality of Preparation to Meet Real Systems Needs

In preparing and carrying out a major systems change, smaller companies tend to fall short in systems design and documentation while larger companies tend to overdesign and document to the point that revision may be more costly than necessary. However, most companies, both large and small, lack quality of design and documentation, basically because it is more difficult to achieve quality. It is harder to achieve:

1. Knowledge of the true facts,
2. Simplification and clarity in design,

3. Straightforward documentation, including decision tables, and so on.

The things easily available are usually done:

1. Automation of the existing system as it was in the past, with little documentation.
2. Design of a program that has redundancy to satisfy individual desires (but not real needs), because it can thus be sold to various functions more easily.
3. Use of ambiguous statements on logistics that have never been answered clearly before.

Thus, sometimes the easy way is the more verbose and costly; it may not be the best, or the cheapest, or of the highest quality.

10. Data Inquiry and Transmission

Too many data-inquiry and transmission systems designs are dependent on specific hardware and have to be fully automated in order to operate. Frequently, such systems are too costly and create an unnecessary strain on the organization.

The better approach is to consider the desirability of a parallel operation, which will permit the gradual conversion and the use of a compatible manual system in areas where conversion is not economic.

Typical of such areas of inquiry, data collection, and transmission, a company with 75 branch offices had an order-entry form designed for transmission. Over half of the branch offices could have completed the entry manually and mailed it to headquarters for input at that point if the design had permitted compatible manual entry. Some companies permit interrupt or on-line inquiry in the spares department, but the same inquiry can be made at the console at periodic intervals with less core and main-frame interruption.

Other companies have their data-collection stations at the most important and highly used places, and have other areas use a modified format on which they can send batch entries to a central station. Making such alternatives available takes slightly longer in the beginning, but usually saves time and cost in the end.

Disk Access versus Tape

While it is risky to forecast ahead in the computer field, we tend to see the following pattern in the future use of disk versus tape access:

Small-Job Shops	Disk only
Large-Job Shops	Disk main; tape for history
Small High-Production Shop	Tape only
Large-Production Shops	Tape main; Disk for limited inquiry

Bank	Predominantly batch-processing
Insurance }	on tape; some inquiry
Process industries	on disk

The advent of floppy disks and mass storage devices is making the proper choice less stereotyped.

Originally, we placed greater emphasis on immediate inquiry with disk systems than on any other feature. When some installations managed good batch-inquiry about once an hour, the next advantage seemed to be the easier ability to deal with complex programs. Today the major advantage of disks seems to rest with the ability to expose the various data-base records to the central processor at a single time. This permits the processing of integrated programs with considerably greater ease than with tape systems. The final advantage of disks in complex business systems is partial processing, particularly in updating bills of material and exploding changes in requirements. Disk-file layout must have a proper balance between adequate access and excessive keys, which reduce the amount of the record to be transferred to a portion of a long single file record.

Tape may still predominate in the high impact on records and batch-processing jobs.

11. Broad Planning Backed by Step-By-Step Implementation

While we are advocates of planning broadly and thinking in terms of the total main business information systems, hard experience has shown that the planning to bring too many things on line at one time frequently can result in disaster. It has also been proved, time and again, that the persons likely to overpromise in this regard may be the managers of the data center themselves, who are eager to support their position by meeting a deadline conversion date.

In one case the managers responsible for two divisions tried to implement programs simultaneously on the same computer. The systems managers and the consulting group felt that such a double load might be disastrous, even though the systems design and the actual debugging of the programs could be accomplished in parallel by increasing the staff related to this particular function. A senior staff manager convinced the president that by moonlighting the programming and by increasing the testing on outside computers, the objective could be accomplished. The moonlighting was inadequate; the concentration of the systems staff to make up for this deficiency meant that the first program described in the section above floundered even more than it might have without this additional load. In actual fact, the second system took priority, was debugged, and became rather effective, while the effort that had gone into the first system was now a lost investment. This is not necessarily so in the systems design or programming supported by independent task forces. The real problem seems to lie with both the actual application being made and the demands placed against the same group. Management should have good error control and reporting, so they can determine whether the application is likely to result in success or failure.

Regardless of how widely conceived, how widely designed a business system may be, the applications should proceed in manageable subsystems, and the responsible executive concerned should be assured of having information as to the rate of progress in correcting data during the application. Thus informed, he can curtail portions of the application, or add additional forces to bring it under control within a reasonable period of time. (In almost every major conversion to computer application, the long hours result in haggard faces for the personnel involved in this rather exciting task.) The people involved with such a strenuous undertaking are so far into the forest that they become the least capable of making a judgment as to how to get out of the woods. It is only by having outside managers with indices of success or failure as each day progresses, that these situations can be dealt with effectively.

F. DIFFICULTIES ENCOUNTERED IN LARGE COMPANIES

Another myth of management is summed up in this recently published statement: "Large companies are ahead in computer applications and will continue to lead the way." Although it is true that many large companies have made substantial strides in applying computers to integrated business systems, the political and interfunctional problems encountered in trying to integrate a large company are formidable.

At one large electronics company, we met with forty executives for our first planning meeting. One group debated for several hours over the wisdom of proceeding at all. When this political roadblock was resolved in favor of going ahead, the meeting proceeded at half the normal pace, with groups of five to ten people involved in the interfunctional discussions. The first meeting was typical of the entire project. Innumerable delays were caused by interfunctional disputes and people's inability to work together.

Companies in the $25 to $150 million sales bracket find integration easier to accomplish; and with proper leadership they can advance more rapidly and achieve better return on investment in a shorter time. These companies have tight control and a flexibility of response to changing conditions which give them an enviable competitive position.

The problems of developing and installing an integrated business system in a large (billion-dollar) corporation are many times the magnitude of those for small concerns. They are, in fact, so great that many predict that large corporations will never have total business systems. Often, the best way to overcome the coordination problem is for the chief executive to sponsor a broad-based survey to develop a master plan. After such a plan gets official approval, implementation may be slow but it has a greater chance of success than before. There are just too many horizontal lines of flow across the multitiered power structure to make the job easy. Without such a survey, it is almost impossible to achieve approval by all departments on the continuous stream of items that require resolution.

The first step in large corporations is to diagnose the number of "total" systems that will be required by the business structure. We argue against those who say that the systems are divided into four or five major areas by function. Rather we suggest that the systems be differentiated by type of product or type of market in large corporations, and that the across-function requirements become an integral part of each system.

Function	Integrated
Engineering	Order entry and distribution
Marketing	Master scheduling
	Material requirements
Production	Scheduling work study
Financial	Accounting, Financial,
Personnel	Personnel

Functional systems design increases the duplication of records, and results in hoarding basic data within each function's control. Thus, a large corporation with products in a single industry might have one total system, while another would require three or four. Within each total system, the four or five major functional areas would be integrated.

A controller of one of the largest corporations once said, "It is so difficult to get systems agreement between exploration, production, and distribution when each of these vertical companies is larger than many total businesses, but there is evidence that we need it every day."

Having defined one area of a large corporation for a total systems survey, it becomes necessary to plan the approach. In one case example, a $200 million industrial-products division was selected, in preference to the larger consumer-item division, because the former offered the greater complexity (50,000 end products by size, 30,000 customers, 10 plants, 7 warehouses). The task force consisted of two consultants, one corporate senior systems analyst, one marketing-division representative, one production representative, one financial representative, and part-time participation from all other functions. One segment of the task force dealt with the order entry, forecasting, requirements planning, distribution, and data communications problems. The other task force was assigned to the production scheduling and work loading subsystems.

The first part of the assignment was to look for profit opportunities related to an information and control system. Here, simulation and sampling is a great tool. Testing was conducted in the following areas:

Forecasting	Work-in-process
Distribution cost and logistics	Scheduling efficiency
Warehouse stock and service rates	Procurement opportunities,
Factory stocks	price breaks, etc.

This phase of the program worked as well as it did in smaller companies but caused far less impact. Contrary to smaller companies, larger ones often prefer to make test applications in areas where control already exists, rather than where the greatest opportunity for significant improvement exists.

The second phase of the investigation was to study the existing system in sufficient detail to spot gaps and duplication. The results were then contrasted with an integrated system, showing the potential dramatic improvement.

The slow pace towards implementation of this unified business system directed attention toward changes in the organizational structure that would enhance the speed of application. The survey had proceeded under a task-force operation which had been successful in providing the communications between the division and the corporate systems and data-processing group. It soon became obvious that the line officials in the division would not readily accept the proposed system if implemented by the corporate systems group. It was considered logical that they would accept more readily the implementation from a senior staff person reporting directly to the divisional manager. When this senior staff person was appointed, it was also necessary to coordinate him with the various functions of the division. The controller for the division suggested that it would be better for such an official to report directly to the division manager rather than through the controller, in order to remove any financial stigma that might be attached to the implementation of the improved systems programs.

As this organization was being created within the division, it was also necessary to consider the inefficiencies of current organization within the systems and data-processing group. This group had been organized along functional lines with a systems manager, a data-center manager, a planning manager, and an operations-research manager, all reporting to the corporate manager of systems and data processing. The systems manager had over 350 systems and programming-type people reporting to him for the entire operation of the corporation. While there were several supervisors within the systems group, coordination with each individual division frequently became bogged down in the higher-level systems and EDP group. Task Force leaders were appointed with a nucleus of systems and programming staff to support the activities. The administrative manager of the division coordinated directly with the Task Force leaders in the appropriate control systems and data-processing group. The corporate manager of systems became more of a staff adviser to the Task Forces.

While these changes improved the operations in this large company, the pace of application of the integrated systems was still substantially behind what it would be in a small company. While the larger corporation has to deal with the more complex problems of compatible file layouts, scheduling the use of the large computers in the data center, and corporate continuity, we believe large corporations can proceed to organize each required total system along these lines. A project team of corporate systems, combined with a divisional group that has the responsibility for successful implementation, will lead to more effective progress.

G. MINICOMPUTERS AND TIME SHARING

Although, in earlier chapters, we have not discussed minicomputers, their rapid development in the 1970–75 period has made available to smaller businesses those benefits described herein that heretofore were available only to their larger brothers.

The lack of complexity in the small business may make the problems described in this book less formidable and, therefore, many small companies may catch up or pass their larger competitors in value received from efforts with computer systems. The exception may be the complex small business that needs a sophisticated "Daily Net Change Material-Requirements Planning System" that requires a midsize computer for proper execution. For these cases another alternative is developing:

- The small on-site Mini for regular programming, backed up by
- A large time-sharing computer for daily batch-processing of a complex "Daily Net Change MRP System."

This combination has an additional benefit in that the daily net change MRP system is costly to develop and program (and even application packages are expensive). However, with time-sharing, the development costs will be shared by many users.

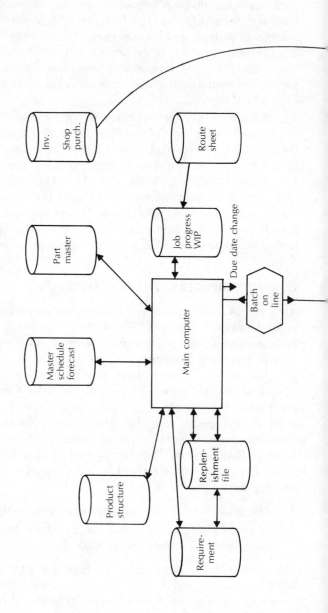

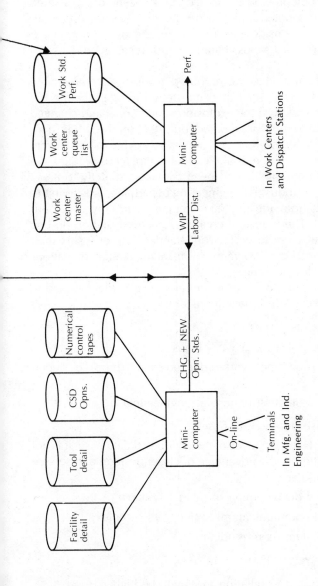

Figure 4.1 Computerized standard data

1. Distributed Data Base

The continued cost reduction in minicomputers and the development of "intelligent terminals" (those that have some memory and recall) have presented a more flexible alternative to the middle- and large-size companies that has not previously existed. In a recent case, a large company experienced a deterioration in results from the large central-computer system. After considerable frustration, the division manager installed a Mini for stock-status balance and receipt- and issue-transactions.

When a new central service was proposed, it wisely accommodated the Mini and its stock-status—and then transferred the data before the daily update of the central files: the explosion of additional and changed requirements and the return of updated priorities to the Mini. This network gave the user close on-line service without having to have a very complex communications system in the central computer as would have been the case if all the terminals had been converted directly to it.

In another case, an industrial engineering department was trying to get improved service from the central computer (currently at 2-hour interval interruptions). The industrial engineers believed that an on-line terminal would permit them to write work standards faster (using their Computerized Standard Data Program), by recalling similar operations through group technology coding.

The network of a combined Mini-central system is diagrammed in Fig. 4.1. The most likely Mini applications are:

- Stock status, receipts, issues
- Job progress, queue lists, and work loads
- Order-entry decision and work-order position (spares or repair orders)
- Operation sheet estimating (industrial engineering)

2. Evaluation of Distributed Data Base

While there are many factors in favor of the distributed data base, it is not all one-sided. In addition to the advantage of closer position and service to user, the Minicomputer can:

1. Permit more rapid development of related systems;
2. Make the central communications system less complex;
3. Make the total system more modular.

On the negative side:

1. The initial design and installation costs will be higher;
2. The equipment costs will be higher forever;

3. It will be more difficult for the EDP and systems manager to maintain design and programming standards in the more remote operations.

It can be pointed out that the Minis in a distributed data base are more of a design concept than a hardware separation alone. A main computer could still carry a large portion of the system and certain redundant files would be assigned to it. All the terminals on the Minis could be connected to this partition. This would allow the Mini to work on its own programs, and the daily transfer of data to the central file and return of the updated information would be handled in a similar fashion. Thus, the key to the design is:

- Are the Mini jobs going to be on-line and all of the complexities of updating and running operational programs faced simultaneously?
- Or are the "on-line" service programs and files going to be batched in and out of the central computer, with easier control of timing and maintenance of records?

We believe most industrial companies can be adequately serviced by the latter at substantially lower costs.

Manufacturing Data Systems (See Appendix D–Directions For The 1980's)

H. SUMMARY

1. A broad-based survey of a total systems area of activity, crossing functional lines rather than being confined to either the marketing, engineering, manufacturing, production distribution, or finance area, is essential to approaching unified business systems effectively.

2. The survey needs only to proceed far enough to outline the overall approach and general areas of opportunity for executive direction toward further study and implementation. The detail advantageous in a smaller company may be a waste of effort in the original stages in a large complex corporation, since after the survey the firm may redirect its approach.

3. A large corporation may require project teams within the corporate systems and data-processing, and an internal divisional organization of an administrative officer and functional representatives who can work with this corporate project group. Otherwise, project administration is likely to be hopelessly delayed by meetings and red tape. Line people within the division should have the implementation responsibility.

4. The successful use of technical people to provide logistical solutions to integrated business problems necessitates a practical exposure to

the conditions existing within the operations; otherwise, the cost and the practicality of results will be questionable. A recent comparison supports this summary quite pointedly. The PIOS program at Jones & Lamson (a Textron company) took 1 systems designer, 2 programmers, and 2 data-control clerks 2½ years with the aid of about one year of consulting. A large manufacturing company (which prided itself in finishing an almost identical Requirements Planning System) used a force of 55 men for over 5 years. Yes, the same results but at about 15 times greater expenditure! Master planning, survey, task forces, and tight control do produce amazing differences.

QUESTIONS

	Poor	Slow	Average	Good	Excellent	Superior
1. Do we really have a Master Plan? How adequate is it?						
2. Have we determined adequate policy statements on cost of money, service performance to customers, acceptable queue lengths in mfg. etc.?						
3. Is our data base properly structured for both now and far enough into the future?						
4. Do we have adequate management-by-exception routines and ones that can adequately bypass an overloaded or aborted section of the system?						
5. Have the users adequately participated in systems specifications?						
6. Have we tested data accuracy?						
7. Do we have adequate data edit routines?						
8. Do we have the staff and timetable for adequate documentation?						

QUESTIONS—Continued

	Poor	Slow	Average	Good	Excellent	Superior

9. Does the plan allow for adequate review after:
   Systems proposal?
   Application description?
   Systems description?
   Design?
   Application?						

10. Have we allowed adequately for the expansion and growth of the system?						

11. Have we adequately reviewed:
   Computer operation systems?
   Data Base Management Systems?
   Applications software?						

12. Is our system sensitive to real needs or does it only give gross controls that aren't a significant improvement over the past?						
13. Is the design modular, so that subsystems can be improved without disrupting the whole?						
14. Have we overkilled with Operations Research and Logistical theory, so that good basic decisions will be confused or overlooked?						
15. Have we put quality vs. sheer time and effort into the system?						

QUESTIONS—Continued

	Poor	Slow	Average	Good	Excellent	Superior
16. Have we adequately considered disk/tape, minicomputers, software, and other factors by checking with successful installations elsewhere?						
17. Does our Master Plan call for broad planning with step-by-step implementation?						
18. If the design is ready, are we willing to have it overviewed by experts before committing to full-scale programming, test, and debugging?						

5
Implementing an MIS System

A. CREATING THE DATA BASE AND IMPLEMENTATION
GUIDES

B. SCHEDULING AND CONTROL OF SYSTEM
CONVERSION

C. SUMMARY

Implementation is not easy, even under the best of circumstances. It is surprising, therefore, how few people do the many little things that can make the implementation process easier. We stressed earlier the need to create a positive environment for change; the title of this chapter might well be "Creating a Favorable Environment for Implementation." The suggestions presented in this chapter will not solve all implementation problems. (Systems people love to quote Murphy's Law: "If anything can go wrong, it will.") However, if we anticipate and provide for some of the more common things that can go wrong, we can make implementation that much easier.

A.   CREATING THE DATA BASE AND IMPLEMENTATION GUIDES

1.   Each Department Responsible for Quality of its Own Data

It is foolhardy to assume that the automation of the present system and/or the use of existing data will be good enough to do the job. In most companies, too little is known about the total method of doing business and too little about the human judgment and intervention that keeps it running. Industry operates in isolated functional or divisional units that are segregated from one another. Functional managers are frequently in the dark as to their own areas, to say nothing of lacking knowledge of the rest of the company. Thus, the automation of the present data and system in an unimproved state may cause substantial damage to the effectiveness of operations. In fact, the computer may make the situation worse. While there is tremendous redundancy in manual systems, frequently the errors may be isolated or averaged; however, in the computer system, each item of data is used and reused—so if it is wrong, the error spreads quickly through many parts of the system. It is best, then, to beware of untested data.

In most major programs, a company must assign *data auditors* at the beginning of design. Even so, this data may turn out to be the critical path in the program, both for application testing and for systems startup.

It is common to find that one requirement of good MIS application is missing; this is a systematic method of tracking down responsibility for poor quality of input data and instituting corrective action. Many systems are in trouble because errors are considered data processing's responsibility, whereas they actually originate from:

Poor engineering bills of material	Inaccuracies in production
Poor routings	departments
Inaccuracies in receiving	Missing records on split jobs
Inaccuracies in the stock room	Inaccuracies in timekeeping

Data processing has neither the responsibility nor the knowledge to correct these errors. Often the managers who complain that data processing produces poor quality are the ones who run the departments that create the greatest difficulty. A functional manager should not place blame too quickly because, if he has not insisted on systematic recording and feedback, the responsibility for data shortcomings may be his own.

A key to achieving improvement in accuracy seems to be the steering committee. The purpose in establishing the steering committee is to clearly define responsibility for making decisions regarding the accuracy-improvement effort. It does not usurp the power of top management but, rather, manages the program and is held accountable for its success. It should be made up of people who (a) have sufficient responsibility to make decisions about everything having to do with the program, with the possible exception of company policy items, and (b) represent the various departments that are most affected by and have the most to gain from inventory accuracy.

After identifying and selecting the steering committee members, an orientation should be conducted where top management expresses its commitment to the effort, sets forth the reasons for establishing the steering committee, and explains how people were selected. Following the orientation, an initial meeting of the steering committee should take place to clarify the role of this group, establish a charter under which they will work, and determine the procedure by which they will attack the problem.

At some point during the initial stages of the steering committee's work, a team-building session is helpful to better enable this group to work together to make decisions and plan.* This can be done in two to four sessions and should be designed to concentrate on issues of leadership, intragroup communication, and identifying blocks to being able to work together.

The steering committee, then, assumes responsibility for solving complex problems with the support of top management. Critical to its success is team-building training. A group expected to work together and to work with others should be given training to better enable them to do

---

*"Some Thoughts on the Use of Cases," Copyright 1972 by Training and Development Systems, Boston, Massachusetts, by Dan Ciampa, Rath & Strong, Inc., p. 2, "open lines of communications between groups of people that had become polarized; build skills in the areas of team development, problem-solving, and effective communications; and help each group learn a systematic planning and problem-solving model that they could apply to the problems that plagued them . . . The second phase of the program was to work together in two groups to analyze a case study of a situation, that was written to demonstrate the need for cooperation in problem-solving activities between groups."

so, just as a competent systems designer needs necessary education to perform his or her task.

2. Support of Costly Data Cleanup

Management, in most cases, never insists on a factual appraisal of the data mess. Without such an appraisal it is a foregone conclusion that the corrective action will be insufficient and inexpertly directed. Corrective action can never be instituted item by item at the point of discovery. Such action is comparable to trying to *inspect* quality into a highly defective product—the only sound solution is to make a highly acceptable product in the beginning.

In some cases, well-intentioned subordinates protect top management. One survey proposal suggested an initial review of bad situations in part-numbering and in bill-of-material control. Members of middle management directed that this be deleted from the proposal on the basis that "top management isn't ready to face a two-year costly improvement program in these areas, and besides they wouldn't understand the problem anyway."

In another case in which top management had supported such cleanup activities, lower-level personnel were protecting each other; "If you don't get your mess cleaned up in a few more weeks, I'll have to tell my boss." These few weeks resulted in 3,000 additional error entries (15% of total) on the stock-status report, all of which could have been dealt with more readily had the boss been told in the beginning.

In striking contrast to these situations are others when, at weekly task-force meetings, the data auditors and the representatives of the various functions give their section's report on the cleanup in each area. In these companies, the size of the problem is known, plans have been carefully prepared to correct the situation, and orderly progress is being made to accomplish the final goals.

3. Minimum Parallel Run for the Duration of Systems Checkout Only

Management must allow a reasonable period for converting from the current to the proposed business system. Such a period must be long enough to identify and correct any major areas of difficulty but short enough that personnel can handle the extra burden of maintaining both the old and new systems. If the workload becomes excessive and extends too long, there is a natural tendency to give priority to the old system.

This principle became obvious in the sixties when a client asked us to help design a computerized inventory-control system involving statistical forecasting, material-requirements planning, economic-order quantities, and statistical reorder points. The system development and data-base preparation proceeded on schedule, and the conversion from a clerical and tab system to a computer-based system started. The client firm agreed that the application should be best followed by a settling-in period for its people. After a short interval they hoped to be in control and ready to start the second phase of the program, which included a new scheduling and workloading system. The consultant assigned to the project stayed through the first few weeks of the implementation, and the normal difficulties that arose were handled with overtime of the regular internal staff. Nothing indicated that any unusual implementation problems would arise during the three months' interval before starting the production-control system. We assumed the client would stop the old system and have the staff concentrate on the new one. In subsequent telephone calls, a variety of reasons were given for not starting the production-control system as scheduled: vacations, availability of key personnel, machine failures, and the like. Finally, six months after the installation of the inventory-control system, one such telephone call revealed *that the client was still operating both systems in parallel.* With this admission, we went back to assist in getting the program back under control. The history of the conversion showed an ever-increasing number of errors in spite of continued progress in making corrections. (This is the major reason why the task forces assigned to computer conversion work such endless hours during the actual transition period.) The strain of maintaining two systems was too much.

After establishing controls on error responsibility, we increased the number of people engaged in corrective action. At the end of two additional months, the outstanding errors had been reduced sufficiently so the conversion to the new system and elimination of the old records could be completed satisfactorily. Our experience in many similar cases indicates that about a four-week parallel run is a good target, with emphasis being placed on correcting system errors rather than individual data errors. Data errors existed in the old system too; and once the strain of running two sysems is over, effective concentration can be devoted to making the *new* single system work effectively.

The manager can learn several things from this part of the story:

- Have a tight schedule for removing the old system, with daily reports on the new system's performance as distinguished from data problems.
- Correct the source of the errors rather than each one separately.
- Have daily reports on data-reject rates with identification of the responsible parties.
- Make the manager who is responsible for the input also responsible for its quality and for the correction, and measure his performance.

4. Insistence on Good Interim Performance of System

One company's approach to unified business systems is included to illustrate three important points.

a)   The inadequacies of the current business system may not permit the uninterrupted development and carefully planned installation of the unified business system. Under these circumstances, the task force assigned to the future development of a unified business system may become integrally involved in improving the current business system to meet today's needs. It is difficult to get line and staff management to accept this involvement initially and to understand the later withdrawal of this support when things are sufficiently under control to permit attention towards development of the future unified business system.

b)   The chief executive has to be able to guide management in an out-of-control situation. Without such top guidance, a company should retreat to simplified systems, even though such action ultimately increases the cost of operations.

c)   Top management must face up to the inadequacies (or insubordination) of key personnel during the application of a unified business system. It is wise to give every manager an opportunity to learn and to develop skill in the use of new systems and control techniques; however, if, after a sufficient period, some cannot adjust to the new methods of operation, they should be replaced. Key managers can err in the direction of replacing managers too hastily, or by deferring an obvious replacement decision far too long.

5. Later Addition of Fancy Steps

Frequently a question arises as to the advisability of starting a reasonably sophisticated business system under a teleprocessing mode or some other complexity. We support the opinion that prevailed in two case studies, that the programs should be developed at each installation using compatible files and programs, with someone in central authority assigned the task of integration. It is then advisable to get the programs underway in each division, either by the use of a separate computer or through the use of a service bureau. When both divisions are satisfied with the operation of the programs, an attempt to put one at the end of a teleprocessing line can be made. This approach, of course, should be modified according to the magnitude of the program and certainly would not apply as fully to warehouses as it would to complex divisions.

6. Minimum Change in Key Personnel during Critical Periods

Changes brought about by a Management Information System tend to create an uncertain environment that requires strong and consistent leadership to see the changes successfully implemented.

Several cases of management changes can be cited, which had a variety of undesirable results:

a)   In one case, the Division Manager was changed frequently; this led to changes in emphasis on support of the Management Information System and in the degree of stimulus towards diversionary programs, with a net effect of at least a year's delay.

b)   In a second instance, a change was made in the office of EDP Manager, and the responsibility for system programming was moved from line to finance; this resulted in about three or four months of renegotiation, definition, etc., before the program could move ahead effectively.

c)   The Materials Manager was promoted to General Manager, and his replacement was ineffective; as a result, there was substantial delay of the system and a bad impact on inventory and shortages.

d)   The Factory Manager was changed during installation; the new manager's lack of interest in the logistics of the proposed system (his philosophy tended toward the old seat-of-the-pants approach) resulted in the gradual decay of the effort.

e)   An otherwise competent Materials Manager failed to recognize plant overloads and take appropriate action. Warned the first time, he was given grace a second—but the third almost cost other managers' jobs as well. The syndrome of watching the details and avoiding the major decision has hurt a substantial number of managers.

The above discussion should not be used as an excuse to avoid crucial changes even at critical times. In some cases, a change in key personnel is deferred too long. Procrastination is easy but almost always wrong. Experience indicates it best to make the change and to support the new executive.

7. Competence of the Manager Must be Tested

Managers must be able to run the system. The up and down history of one company can illustrate this fact very clearly. It concerns one of the earliest computer applications of an inventory and production-control system. The system had reorder points that recognized lead time, safety factors, forecasting techniques, and lot sizing. This system required little overhead and a relatively small amount of programming.

After two years of rather successful application, a new materials manager took over. At this stage, the system started to perform poorly. The number of shortages rose in parallel with sizable increases in inventory, without corresponding increases in shipments. Much of the inventory ended up in subassemblies whose lot sizes were being increased because of savings in manufacturing setup: He could not analyze the inventory buildup in subassemblies, and, even when told how to correct it, could not take the practical steps required. The new manager was replaced by the old. Assembly lot sizes were reduced to one month's quantity, and the system returned to a reasonably effective performance level.

A few years later, another new materials manager added a production scheduling and loading plan to the system. These modifications had barely been implemented when the company again faced a rapid expansion of business. In a short period, the increasing number of shortages indicated that the system was not responding to total output demands. An explosion of the yearly forecast showing expected loads each month did much to project labor requirements and the need to subcontract in critical areas.

This correction program had been underway only a few months when a major new model (1/3% of forecast) had to be replaced in the schedule by an expanded use of the older models. Thus, just as the system was beginning to recover, it was plunged back into an overload condition again. An audit at this point indicated:

- Master scheduling had not been maintained in many model areas.

- In spite of the automated system, the bill-of-material explosion and appropriate order action to all levels still took six weeks (in many cases this was not a significant gain over prior clerical methods).

- Reservations and/or allocations were made too far ahead of actual need, so that it became impossible to differentiate between the items with real stockout risk and those that were primarily paper shortages. (This type of action had been instituted several months earlier by the new manager.)

- There was no matching of shortages at the assembly floor with shortages indicated by the computer system. A consolidated shortage list had to be presented to supervisors and dispatchers to assure effective action.

- Following priorities in fabrication was poor even on known shortages; hot jobs frequently were worked on only during one shift, awaiting a new report the following day. They had received around-the-clock attention under the manual system in the past, but the foreman did not carry this action into the new system.

All of these factors indicate the need to manage the computer-based system as well as to manage the business. Systems provide information and facts for better management. As businesses grow, personnel are promoted and transferred, and less experienced people are assigned roles that may directly affect the use of systems. It is essential to assure that training will be effective if a system is to continue to perform despite management turnover.

An exceptional business systems manager almost "smells" the areas of difficulty because he is sensitive to changes in the new information. This case study has proved to us that "seat-of-the-pants management" has a new connotation. The exceptional business systems manager will develop this type of "feel" about his complex systems in very much the same way that the practical line managers used to have a "seat-of-the-pants feel" about the actual operations itself.

Aftermath

As the major points uncovered by the audit were corrected and a more knowledgeable manager was placed in charge of materials control, the system gradually returned to its original effectiveness. We believe the original materials manager could have run the program effectively through the entire period with substantial savings for the company. The firm will undoubtedly surpass its prior level in the near future. If we ask why systems get out of control, the answer seems to be that materials managers who understand the logic and can respond to the feedback are essential. Computer systems will not run themselves. *The final answers must continue to come from man. The number of managers who really understand and can operate a complex business system is usually small in most companies.* Of the two or three that have such competence, the key spot is usually held by the materials manager (production and inventory-control manager), because he can combine knowledge of the business with knowledge of the new system. *Top management must be sure to have the right person in this crucial spot.*

B.   SCHEDULING AND CONTROL OF SYSTEM CONVERSION

1.   Development of a Reasonable Schedule

It is easy for EDP groups to become overloaded; sometimes their situation gets to be worse than that of the factories they are trying to help. In many cases, this is not for lack of effort on the part of competent and interested people. Why, then, does this happen? First, consider the systems programming area.

a)   The biggest single time loss occurs in the period between the completion of programming on all elements, and the point at which the system is operational. The major factors usually are:

  • Losses in coordination and training and a lessening of acceptance of the system. Many of these are difficult to document, but often a visible difference in attitude sets in, between the time when the users eagerly accept the program, and the point at which obvious reluctance exists when it has to be used.

- Poor data running through the system leads to unsatisfactory results, and causes a greater loss because of time spent debugging than would be attributed to the poor data alone.
- Systems and programming people seem to be less effective when they get to the program assembly and implementation phase. The programs have to meet rigorous perfection standards just to operate at all.

These things affect the start of the next assignment, and the overloads build up.

b) Not enough time is allowed for demands from prior programs. Maintenance work can be estimated more accurately, but in most cases enough time is not allowed.

c) Most managers do not realize how low the performance of the newer or poorer people on the staff may be. The range in output can vary by a factor of six; this means that if the estimate is based on *good* performance and the actual output is only *average*, a substantial gap in performance can develop.

Greater managerial talent in interfacing between managers effectively at implementation time is needed. In estimating, managers should know the past performance of each man and do a better job of performance handicapping.

Scheduling the Computer Center

Poor scheduling of the computer center frequently comes from the lack of skill in conventional techniques. In this area, the larger companies frequently do a much better job than the smaller ones. Everyone has problems of equipment breakdown, training, illness, and new-program tests; but, here again, the better managed facilities recover more quickly, while the poorer never return to schedule.

The important elements seem to be:

a) Be sure to have second- and/or third-shift operations that are quickly expandable.

b) Establish relations with a service bureau, or an agreement to exchange computer time with a neighbor that can help in a period of difficulty.

c) Plan to use the second or third shift as the real processing shift, when there will be few interruptions. Programmers and test shots will be scheduled best during the day, even though longer test runs should be on the off shifts.

d) Have work-measurement standards for each job broken down by operations.

e) In all areas, maintain a thorough schedule, keep people well informed, and follow with a frank feedback and discussion of schedule problems and difficulties. Know which jobs have priorities and which ones can be delayed and by how much. From these communications, improved scheduling success may develop.

2. Practical Debugging Experience in Analysis of MIS Problems

In one case study, the efforts of many intelligent computer people were frustrated by the lack of two important considerations in systems design and development. The conversion of their inventory and production control system to computers covered approximately a three-year period and, according to management, expenditures of three-quarters of a million dollars. At the time the situation was appraised, confusion reigned, and management believed they had received no benefit from all of this effort. They relied upon support from the computer hardware manufacturer and from some accounting-type personnel, as well as from their internal staff. All had failed to produce satisfactory answers.

A brief survey over several days resulted in the following important factors being established:

a) *Duplication in ordering of purchased and manufactured parts*

There are advantages to the reorder-point type of ordering in some cases and material-requirement planning in others. Systems designers have to be careful that the logic does not get improperly intermixed. When both types of system are employed, the reorder point should equal only the safety stock, as the requirements during the lead-time period are covered by actual reservations. The ROP is for spare parts protection only.

In this case the reorder point covered the usage during the lead time, and reservations were made as well. This caused a doubling of open orders, and the resulting flood of work made it difficult to expedite shortages. Work-in-process inventory rose rapidly as shipping performance fell off. When the top executives learned of this analysis after many prior false reports on the problem, there was much consternation about previous efforts at correction. The correction of this problem resulted in immediate relief to the shop; however, the real shortages still took a few months to clean up.

b) *Overloading the manufacturing and purchasing capacity*

While the manufacturing manager and purchasing agent must share the blame because they were not more realistic in reporting that new employees or new vendors would not be effective in making a 50 percent expansion in a year's time, higher management should recognize initial failures and provide the proper adjustment to keep the system in balance. There is a philosophy, when sales orders climb rapidly they are piled into manufacturing, which leads to "heap scheduling." Some managers believe the overload will stimulate manufacturing action to accomplish the desired result. In relatively small increases, this may be true, but usually heap scheduling leads to catastrophe when the increase is of the size described above. Well-operated computer systems flounder when overloaded and when management has been ineffective in taking action on the trouble signals.

The best way to deal with these situations is to use a well-planned master schedule that shows total requirements, departmental required hours, and purchase requirements, needed to meet the projected volume of business. In this situation under discussion, the calculation of input–output balances and reduction of the master schedule to the proper level brought the production planning into proper focus, and permitted the successful handling of more gradual increases.

c)   Lack of timely issues maintain accurate on-hand balances

A brief survey indicated that the on-hand balances were very inaccurate, but—worse than this—the timing of receipts, issues, and posting made it both difficult and expensive to verify the records. Many companies pre-issue from the records before sending the data into the shop, and then assume the correct action is going to take place. In a complex situation this always leads to serious record inaccuracies; in simple situations the differences in methods are less significant.

Other companies post transactions so erratically, and so long after the action, that the reconciliation of what is in the pipeline is impossible. Revising the procedure here to post-issue and to batch-control paperwork by a time deadline resolved the situation rapidly. The second step was to raise the job level for receiving and stockroom personnel, so that department did not continue to be a transient training ground for the new employees on their way to the next job level. Inventory accuracy is of sufficient monetary and profit significance that the record-keeping cannot be left to junior employees. Many companies underrate the stores-keeping job in terms of its impact on company operations.

3.   Accurate Development and Testing of New Information Requirements

The new system may require a fair amount of new information that was not collected previously. This new information makes it difficult to check past records for an estimate of the accuracy involved—job-progress records, time reporting, detail requirement records, and separation of usage into new and repair categories. Information may be reported some new way, or by using mechanisms that did not exist in the past. There is a risk that new information will not be dealt with properly where management or clerical employees have made judgments affecting the flow and control of business information without proper documentation. Typical examples are unauthorized substitutions of products, groupings of various orders, informal advance warnings on changes, or carelessness in checking specifications from one function to another. These events may bypass the old business system and create a vacuum in the development of the new business system.

While there are many such situations, it is sufficient to point out that care is required in the advance preparation and testing of a major systems conversion. The manager involved must be aware of the need to follow up, and must be critical about the rate of progress in getting the system implemented and coming to a reasonably quick point of eliminating the old system. Such action permits all efforts to be devoted toward the successful installation and record-keeping for the new business system. Successful brief conversion periods are needed in computer installations to replace the long periods of confusion that take place.

4. Duplication during Partial Phase-Over

One of the most difficult problems in converting from a segmented system to an integrated system is the partial duplication during the phase-over. While it is wise to implement step by step, rarely does one step in an integrated program completely wipe out an equal portion in the segmented system.

Consequently, at the outset, the segmented system may continue in full operation. After a significant portion of the new has been applied, then it may be necessary to develop special programs directed toward eliminating major portions of the old system. This can be accomplished by reprogramming the few items of data that are in the old system but not yet compensated for by the new system. Sometimes advancing a portion of the new system, ahead of schedule, can help in the elimination of a major segment of the old system.

After a substantial portion of the integrated system has been installed, the discontinuation of the remaining segments of the old reaches a greater pace, and it is not unlike going downhill after a tough climb.

5. Redundancy

The vast majority of second-generation systems have a substantial amount of redundancy in their operations. It used to be said that, prior to the computer age, the part number and description could be manually copied 30 to 40 times during a year of business operation. Many people hoped that the computer would easily reduce this to a single entry—or at least a few entries—into the system. Not so. We estimate the partial duplication of input and stored data to be in the 5 to 10 range. This is because the several functions of the average business create independent demands, and at varying time intervals, upon the systems group. Limited attempts at compromise to more highly integrated systems produce only modest success. Thus, much opportunity still remains.

Many managers are unaware of the degree to which redundancy still exists. One manager who had been told that he had a highly integrated and computerized system was shocked to find that, within the computer room, he still had as many as 13 partial duplicate entries and card handling and re-entry of cards to make the system operate properly. A change in sequence, or the scrambling of the 5,000–10,000 cards on a single shift, could produce a nightmare that would require weeks of recovery. We encourage managers to ask for an audit of this data-handling situation on a periodic basis. In this way, management can be assured of a gradual improvement.

In one situation, a manager asked for a higher-speed computer with larger core and a mass storage device before such was really needed. Concern was expressed whether this would be used as a crutch to read card images in and then transfer to modified programs to run from the card images. Such a step would reduce card processing substantially and increase speed, because the slow input for the re-entry of the card would be eliminated. Such a step may be wise if it is a temporary crutch and is not allowed to forestall true simplification and integration of the system.

6. Need for Friendly Realistic Review

In many computer installations the unfavorable attitudes toward a new system are created during the issue of the initial output. Frequently, obvious mistakes or omissions, which are readily noticeable to the line people, get into circulation. Usually, this type of error can be corrected rather quickly, but the damage may live a long time thereafter.

Most of this difficulty can be eliminated by getting the first output reviewed in the data center by one or two friendly managers from the line organization. They are usually flattered at being asked and are frequently concerned that a worthwhile system could be aborted if current errors are not corrected.

Total time is frequently saved by putting the first period of output to the torch rather than releasing it to the users, thus taking more time to get the output in excellent shape for a deferred release to the users' group.

7.   Maintain Checking Ahead of the Users

Even after the first few rough spots have been handled properly, it is unsafe to assume that output will be satisfactory until things have settled down to a well established routine. During this period it is wise to continue to sample-check the output before it goes to the users. One can think of several kinds of odd conditions.

- Some input cards omitted.
- Cards incomplete.
- Programs out of sequence.
- Previous rejected transactions are voluminous and not resolved.

When the output is poor, it is to the credit of the data center to catch it first, and either rerun or skip the day's report. This follows the rule that "misinformtion may be worse than no information." This rule is related to the extra cost of correcting poor action, rather than the mere delaying of proper action.

Complete critical analysis by the users

In some cases the users give a cursory look at output, finding enough wrong with it to cause rejection. Weeks later problems are still coming from the user, not because they are new, but because they have become noticeable now that the more obvious problems have been cleared away.

The whole debugging period could have been shortened and handled with less cost if the users had made a very exhaustive study at the outset. Sometimes this can be accomplished best if the systems analyst and the user go through the detail together.

8.   Primary Attention To Payback Areas

The payback in the application of integrated business systems may be in the areas of the greatest complexity. Systems efforts short of this point in some situations may not be worthwhile as a return on the investment.

One case study involves a company that had an early development of the use of punch-card equipment for accounting, inventories, status, and loading reports. It is of significance in terms of both the case study and the fact that people frequently do not get the full utilization from the equipment.

A survey was made of potential opportunity for further development of this system, and the simulations indicated a sufficient operating savings to justify the cost of going to a medium-sized computer. The survey indicated that the application of priority-of-scheduling rules, such as critical ratio, and the installation of time-phase master scheduling and requirements planning would produce the necessary savings to give a substantial payback on the cost of installation and future operation of the computer. Once the program was underway, however, corporate head- quarters desired to integrate this program with that of a sister division to attempt to bring these programs along in parallel. Considerable effort was made to convince the local management that these sophisticated programs were not necessary and that the whole installation should continue along much simpler lines. The local management, however, continuously pointed out that the simpler installation would offer them none of the improvement beyond what they had in the original tab system; for this reason they felt that they should not be held responsible for the return on the investment in the program or the payback from the computer. The consultant's opinion finally prevailed and after a substan- tial amount of interdivisional discussion to reach compatible files for future benefit, the program was permitted to proceed as originally scheduled.

C.   SUMMARY

Implementation is where it all pays off. All of the time and investment up to this point will be wasted if the system cannot be made operational. Some systems run in parallel for years and never do replace the existing one. Other systems are replaced, but the new one performs less adequately than the old.

The points made in this chapter aren't a cure-all, but they can go a long way towards helping when followed.

QUESTIONS

	Poor	Slow	Average	Good	Excellent	Superior
1. Have we insisted that each department be responsible for its own data?						
2. Do our edit routines and audit trails reflect an ongoing test of data accuracy by input source?						
3. Is management committed to support data cleanup down through the lower levels?						
4. Is the parallel operation (if any) adequately planned, of short duration, and geared to feedback?						
5. Will management demand and force a good intermediate performance of the system?						
6. Is there a commitment to stability in the key departments during changeover?						
7. Is management ready to deal with incompetence or inexperience and to make moves to overcome such problems?						
8. Does our conversion schedule appear reasonable?						
9. Do we have adequate systems, program, and user debugging personnel assigned? Will we test in all of these areas?						

QUESTIONS—Continued

	Poor	Slow	Average	Good	Excellent	Superior
10. Are we geared to the necessary duplication during phaseover?						
11. Is the degree of redundancy justified?						
12. Will we get a realistic review from the users before we play for keeps?						
13. Is our implementation focused in the best payback areas?						
14. Have we adequately explored and selected the outside expertise that we would engage if serious trouble develops?						

6

Living With An MIS System

A. GENERAL COMMENTS
B. PROFITS DURING TRANSITION

A. GENERAL COMMENTS

Complacency is the most insidious enemy of the successfully designed and implemented MIS. The tendency to sit back, view the accomplishment with justifiable pride, and let the system run itself must be overcome. No system runs itself; the system is only as effective as people make it, after implementation as well as before.

1. Management's Responsibility for Overall Controls and Policy Determination

MIS does more than solve specific logistical problems. It provides management with the ability to implement broad policies for governing the overall effectiveness of the company's operations.

One company, for example, adjusts the value of the money in the inventory formula to make inventory policy respond to the general forecast and the financial judgment of top management. Its products are machine tools that are subject to capital goods cycles. A decrease in the value of money in the Economic Order Quantity (EOQ) formula permitted a better proration of setups and the building of the inventory at the right time *ahead* of the increased sales in the machine tool industry. As the capital goods cycle reached a subsequent peak, management increased the money value and obtained the corresponding reduction in inventory. At the end of a boom period, a one-year's inventory at a high volume of sales could suddenly become two to three years of inventory at lower volume levels. Keeping inventory in a proper relationship to the volume of sales during such declines requires that input be much lower than shipments. The labor force must also go below the declining sales curve and then recover. Failure to adjust early in the cycle necessitates greater adjustment in the long run.

2. Time Needed to Achieve Projected Savings

In one installation a manufacturing manager commented on the Master Plan, "You didn't leave me any reaction time." At the end of a two-year installation period of a new integrated inventory, production-control, and priority-scheduling system, the savings had been projected to start accumulating immediately. The manager said, "When I get this information, my work just begins; I need to make tools and machines more flexible, make operators more flexible, educate my supervisors on how to make new decisions, use more alternate routings, etc. I want the program, but I need enough reaction time to maintain a positive attitude in my group—not a feeling that we're behind schedule and under the gun." He won.

3. Effective Use of the System by Managers

Managers who are responsible for the control and override of a computer-based business system must understand clearly the strengths and weaknesses of such systems. Overriding the system when it is providing the best answer, or failing to override the system when it cannot provide the best answer, may produce equally disastrous situations. One company, which makes many small tools, had several large annual orders for substantial amounts of business. While the manager responsible did sense that it was advisable not to enter these orders as one huge annual requirement, his decision to split them into thirds, rather than into monthly increments, threw the logistics off base. The action in this case made the system relatively ineffective for a period of months. This system, in fact, had control limits on the forecasting that would have immediately identified the attempt to include these large orders, had the management override not taken place.

It is equally important for managers to recognize when the system cannot respond quickly enough. One of the followup audits in the company mentioned above indicated such a situation. A review of items that had a high incidence of stockout indicated that a single large issue had dragged down the available inventory, and then a continuing higher incidence of demand over a period of several months had never permitted the replenishment system to catch up. This system had adequate control reports indicating repeat stockout performance and all of the necessary information upon which managers could make judgments to improve the system. The manager should have put in an extra order or an increased quantity even if such had to be subcontracted outside to return stability and reduce the high stockout rate.

4. Maintenance of Flexibility

There is valid criticism that an efficient production-scheduling system with minimum work-in-process leaves little flexibility in the assembly or shipping program for replacement of parts due to cancellation, scrap, or failure at test. The sound plan is to overschedule carefully, so that units can be called forward if such an incident occurs. This overschedule should not be cumulative but should be constantly adjusted to the desired fill-in capability. Handled in this manner, a 10 percent increase in work-in-process inventory could provide the flexibility that a 50 percent or more excess frequently provides today.

In several case studies, the failure to make shipments in total dollars resulted in costly panics at month's end to ship everything possible. This left the assembly floor dry at the beginning of the next month and created substantial excess cost in that month also. The new scheduling systems, with the planned 10 percent overschedule, eliminate the prior costly procedures and loss in profit due to the fear of low shipments.

5. Good Effects Overridden by Managerial Bulls

The "Bull of the Woods" managers are found at all levels of the organization. They "do their own thing" regardless of their impact on operations. Here are a few examples that we have seen.

- A factory manager releases all orders to the shop even though they are beyond the lead time (heap scheduling);

- A production-control supervisor does not maintain an audit on his order-release box, and orders are issued very late;

- Foremen and dispatchers do not follow priority list or check for permission to deviate from the list;

- An EDP manager delays 10 weeks in reporting a buildup of noncleared exceptions in the inventory section;

- An order clerk forgets orders that he placed in his drawer;

- A president insists on accepting order deliveries to meet an impossible schedule;

- A factory manager splits lots unnecessarily and destroys the value of the EOQ's;

- A manager overrides the statistical forecast and is wrong 27 times out of 30;

- An engineering-section leader says the unit is released on time but has to add 20 percent through memos at a much later date.

Every company should maintain an honest list of its own problem areas. The task force should rank these in terms of importance of corrective action. Eventually the whole standard of operation can be raised to a new high performance level.

6. Actual Operations Reflected by Data

There must be a real-life relationship between the data in the computer-based system and what is actually taking place in real operations. In one of the first case studies for a complex business application, the bills of material (as described by the Engineering Department) had a structure that was substantially different from those used in the actual manufacture of subassemblies and assemblies in the plant. Engineering structured their bills in a geographical sense, listing those parts in each subassembly drawing in accordance with their relationship to the function of that particular part of the mechanism. Manufacturing, on the other hand, had regrouped these parts in many cases so that the subassembly could be

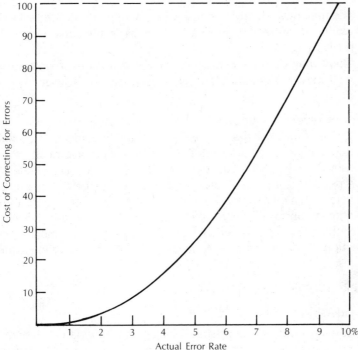

Figure 6.1

made without all of the connecting parts. (In other cases it may be best for manufacturing to exclude items from a subassembly to compensate for left or right-hand, or other unique variations. Omitting these parts from subassembly lists provides greater flexibility in using these subassemblies when the specific configurations of the customer orders become firm.)

A managerial meeting to determine the program of reconciliation was never supported and resulted in ordering parts in different groups than those in which they were used. At the final assembly of the major unit, some items stocked out, causing a damaging effect on deliveries. In addition, attempts to verify the actual balance on hand with the action that had supposedly taken place within the computer became hopelessly confusing.

7. Need for Exceptional Performance

Only in rare instances are computer systems pushed to the point of excellence. there appear to be several reasons for this.

a) The relief that comes from being as successful as others and better than many takes management's eye away from the full potential.

b) The final push will have the biggest effect upon clerical replacement, and this creates uneasiness.

c)   The final push should also result in system performance that reduces workload at technical levels, such as expeditors, order clerks, buyers, etc.

d)   There may be some subconscious fear that if the programs run too well, past performance may appear worse than it was.

Equally important to the personnel reduction achieved as a result of quality of a system, is the ability to run the business on facts rather than on "feel." The results rise dramatically as the quality of the data goes above 95 percent. If the cost of correcting poor data rises geometrically, then the curve shown in Fig. 6.1 would develop. Thus a 2 percent error rate would cost 4 percent; a 4 percent rate, 16 percent; a 7 percent error rate could drop rejects to a 49 percent, and error rates greater than 10 percent might make any manpower savings difficult. There is logic to this, because the higher the error rate, the greater the manpower requirements for data correction, and there is a greater need to rely on alternate manual-support systems.

B.   PROFITS DURING TRANSITION

1. Leadership

Almost every study of successful Management Information Systems has placed top management participation at the top of the list of "reasons for success." This is true, but it does not go far enough. First, there is a wide range of variation on the success side. *Some companies achieved that goal only after extreme difficulties in implementation, while others had programs that contributed to profitability all during the installation.** Second, there are cases where top management supports without follow-up and control, as compared to other top management teams who participate and are insistent on results. For example, we have often heard these statements:

a)   We can't correct our data until the program is in operation.

b)   We can't control inventory until we get good scheduling and loading.

c)   We can't reduce work-in-process inventory and early pickups until everything is perfect.

d)   We will be six months behind schedule because we don't have the people.

e)   The engineering and manufacturing bills of material should be properly coded and should agree, but we can't afford to straighten them out.

The good general manager sees through these comments to the solutions

---

*See Appendix 2—both Nordberg and Jones & Lamson improved performance while reducing staff.

that lie behind. He insists from the start that people deal with the hard problems that won't go away; he focuses on correcting the "A" problems so that the resources are not squandered in gaining correction; he ensures that functional managers are concerned with detailed performance within their operations, which they might prefer to ignore. This type of leadership is more than supportive; it is participative and insistent.

2. Avoiding Catastrophes

Perhaps the second most important thing that leadership can do is avoid an out-of-control situation. Almost every difficulty can be dealt with successfully and in time, except a situation that gets out of control. Experience indicates that it is far easier to get out of control than to return to that happy state.

If the reasons for being out of control were listed, poor data would be on top for everyone. But this statement is too simple—the data was probably even less accurate prior to computerization, yet there was a semblance of control in those earlier days. The difference is that, coupled with the poor data, there is the sense of being lost in the new situation that did not exist in the prior one. The new system forces us to rely on new reference points, while the old reliable ones have been changed or destroyed. In some cases, the old reference points may still be there, but people have forgotten how—or don't dare—to use them.

Another data problem is simply speed. Poor data brought rapidly to management for action may produce a quick, and possibly erroneous decision, whereas poor data moving slowly and averaged into longer reporting periods in the old manual system gave management time to reflect and allowed errors to cancel one another.

The second reason for being out of control is loading facilities beyond capacity because of poor master scheduling. Even systems that have been automated successfully may flounder under such conditions. Warnings of overload and high shortages may continually be directed to management for action—but these can be ignored. Many managements have a history of being mesmerized into the belief that they can handle everything on schedule when sales volume goes up substantially. Some managers who paid attention to capacity problems under the manual system convince themselves that the computer will solve these problems, and thus do not insist on good master scheduling.

Another source of catastrophe is lack of knowledge and training. In a few cases we have found the data to be adequate and the master scheduling in reasonable control, but people do not follow the rules. Typical examples are where production and inventory control supervisors:

a)   Release requirements far ahead of lead time;
b)   Do not review the suspense order file to release jobs on time;

c)   Do not work the jobs in proper priority sequence in the plant;
d)   Take override action that wipes out good controls in the system;
e)   Build large quantities of subassembly lots without understanding the impact on total inventory and shortages; or
f)   Design a full reservation system on top of ROP system, resulting in double ordering.

This list could be expanded, but it is more important to discuss some of the causes. Surveying many management-information systems installations, we find only two or three managers per company that fully comprehend the operation of the system. This small number is not always because of lack of exposure; probably less than 25 percent of the people exposed really develop a working understanding of the system. Such understanding requires the unique combination of:

a)   Knowledge of the business.
b)   Knowledge of the logistics used.
c)   Knowledge of how the system operates.

For this reason most managements are asked to increase the participation of key people in the task force during installation, but they do not. Yet it becomes one of their principal concerns a few years later.

The number of supervisors at lower levels who fully understand their roles varies. Some understand very well and can partially compensate for deficiencies in others. But here the "weakest link" theory applies. One poor performer substantially reduces the effectiveness of the whole operation. The deficiency in training stems primarily from lack of on-the-job follow-up. Supervisors can repeat all the rules in the classroom, but applying these to a wide variety of situations that have been handled by habit is a different problem. Even on-the-job training is not enough; the manager must continually check actual performance in each area and get people involved and committed to the system.

The final significant catastrophe problem, one which we have continually addressed in earlier chapters, is that of uncooperative functional managers. If one or more functions is more concerned with suboptimizing its own objectives than with supporting the Management Information System, the disruption can lead to catastrophe.

3.   Short-Interval Plans and Accomplishments

This book places heavy emphasis on long-range planning for Management Information Systems; this should not be interpreted as lack of concern for short-range plans and accomplishments. Too many companies have five-year plans that are elegant, but their relevance to current operation is obscure. Companies that devote an equivalent amount of attention to relating subsystem plans to current operations make more realistic progress. These short-interval plans can frequently be directed toward practical improvement and savings. Typical of these areas are:

a) Improvement of basic data that may make current decisions better.

b) Use of logical rules on a manual basis on "A" parts.

c) Modification of existing programs to support a more meaningful operation while still moving toward the ultimate program. In one company an interim report tying high-level requirements to re-plenishment orders broke bottlenecks and improved expediting several years ahead of the Master Plan. In another, a special interim program produced critical-ratio scheduling years ahead of plan.

d) Elimination of unnecessary reports. In one company it was possible to eliminate a stock-status report that had been a parallel run for three years at an increased cost. The time saved was devoted to a revised design that effectively replaced the manual inventory system.

e) Clarification of policies on where and when to order, lot sizes, price-breaks forecasting, and master scheduling can improve interim results.

These steps are all directed toward keeping the management information system in touch with reality.

4. Necessity versus Luxury

This book does not support the "keep it simple rule," because one of the main advantages of the computer is to deal efficiently with complexity. Nevertheless, we wish to make a case for necessity versus luxury in terms of management information systems.

a) It may be a necessity to have production queue lists updated daily.

It may be a luxury to do this updating on a real-time rather than a batch basis.

b) It may be a necessity to have a second- and third-shift data-center operation to get last night's closing in the morning's opening status reports.

It may be a luxury to have enough computer capacity to handle the total load on a one-shift basis.

c) It may be a necessity to have exception reports reviewed daily.

It may be a luxury to permit a batch of clerks to review all transactions before taking action.

d) It may be a necessity to clean up sources of data error.

It may be a luxury to assign people to work on analyzing and revising each individual entry.

5.   Investment in the Future

Many managements have a general feeling that their investment in MIS systems is for future returns; that is, they admit to no current operating savings, so the rationale must be a future return. Most of these managers would not accept such a fuzzy analysis in any other activity. The excuse offered is "nonaccounting EDP systems cannot be cost-justified." Experience has shown that the EDP operating systems can be based upon cost and savings estimates, and the payback is usually of a magnitude several times greater than that experienced in the accounting areas.

The complexity and total time required for the development and installation of MIS usually runs into several years. The costs of installation are high; the cost of retraining can be high. These factors make it essential to have accurate cost and savings estimates, a Master Plan, and regular management reviews. In this way the subapplications and the expected savings can be monitored along the way, and the breakeven point achieved as early as possible.

6.   Keeping Programs under Control

The final myth is that *computer-supported systems "run themselves."* In fact, any system is only as good as its design, the data available to it, and the people who make it work. Management has to understand the system and take corrective action when the system gets out of control.

Time and again our investigations of companies who cannot live with MIS disclose the following:

a)   A new inventory system has been running in parallel with the manual records for over two years, and no decision has been made to drop either. Most people still rely on the old system.

b)   An attempt at exploding requirements has been made, but the programs are not operational because the bills of material are wrong. No cleanup activity has been started.

c)   The new inventory system has been installed, but inventory has increased, shipments are lower, and accuracy of records is poor. No one knows why.

The surprising things in all of these cases, are the length of time the trouble has existed and the amount of excess cost incurred during such periods. What should have been done?

Keeping programs under control is the answer. The following rules will be of substantial help.

a)   Sample the data for accuracy, and apply corrective action long before systems application. Continue sampling after implementation.

b) Test both programs and system before final application.
c) Delay full operation if the above are not satisfactory.
   Classify errors by major categories, and go to the source to eliminate them.
e) Focus on major systems errors during the first month; do not get bogged down in minor errors.
f) Eliminate the old system after correcting major errors.
g) Apply full manpower to error correction. Give this priority over keeping the old system alive.

7. Rate of Change

The rate of change that is best for any company is highly variable. What appears slow to one company could be disastrous in another. The first word of caution is "Don't exceed your own best rate of change," to be followed quickly by "If your current best rate is too slow—do something about it." When a company exceeds its own acceptable rate, personnel become panicky, confidence is reduced, and time is spent on discussing the situation rather than getting the job done. The end result is not only slower completion but poorer quality as well.

What improves the acceptable rate of change? A management climate in which:

a) People are not blamed for initial mistakes in a new environment.
b) People are rewarded and praised if changes are successfully implemented rapidly and if they are involved in the process.
c) People associated with change are more likely to be promoted.
d) Changes are explained ahead of time at all levels.
e) People creating roadblocks to change are discovered and transferred, if they don't react positively.

8. Maintenance of a Positive Attitude

This is the best note on which to end this chapter: Change can be thrilling, not threatening. Books can be written on techniques, on management, on profit and loss, but they all come to naught if a positive attitude toward change cannot be maintained. While one can point to companies that have succeeded without this ingredient, how much more would they have prospered had they maintained a positive attitude towards change and a faster pace had been possible?

Far more important than exact dollars and cents is the job satisfaction and the sense of accomplishment that comes with successfully handling new situations. While there is some satisfaction in doing a good routine job, the great sense of accomplishment that results from successfully meeting a real challenge is far more rewarding.

QUESTIONS

	Poor	Slow	Average	Good	Excellent	Superior
1. Do our managers have adequate overall controls so that they can sense major factors independently from the new system?						
2. Have we allocated enough run-in time before holding managers responsible for savings and benefits?						
3. Are managers adequately trained in how to use and react to systems output? Are managers instructed regarding factors they ought to keep stable, vs. the ones to be used for close control?						
4. Are managers ready for last-minute failures?						
5. Are our overall signals watched so that catastrophies can be avoided?						
6. Do we have specific short-term tasks continuously in front of managers and task forces?						
7. Can we keep programs under control by inspecting base causes and not correcting all the little individual defects?						
8. Is management geared to keeping a positive attitude while operating under difficulty?						
9. Are we geared to major decisions (if necessary) to maintain control and a successful implementation?						

7
In The Future

A.   CHANGES IN MANPOWER REQUIREMENTS

1.   Training and Management Evolution for the Future

The rate of change and training requirements will be greater in the future than ever before. The effect of maintenance on automated facilities and meeting schedules will also require increased attention. Quality control, industrial engineering, and materials handling may also have impact on the schedule that will have to be more closely controlled. While the new middle-management executive will have a better understanding of the entire operation, he must also be more responsive to carrying out his portion of the total plan.

This does not mean that the middle manager will be a robot in relationship to the planning and operating of his portion of the business. It means rather that his planning contribution will be made in relation to how the business will function next month, and next year (rather than day to day), based upon his analysis and study. The new inputs for improved performance and control will be submitted to the information and control system and merged with the factors from other segments of the business, to update the operating-control plan continually, so that it can achieve low cost and improve quality and performance. The middle-management group will be motivated to do a better job tomorrow in contrast to the more routine job required today, in which they deal with only a portion of the system or operations at any one time.

2.   Greater Emphasis on Prevention of Breakdowns

In dealing directly with plans and schedules coming from the integrated information and control system, the middle-management executive will attempt to achieve a high degree of throughput based on continuous high-quality operation. To obtain this, he will need to have a maximum amount of intelligence regarding points where breakdowns or interruptions could occur that might cause a lack of efficiency in production or the manufacture of off-quality goods. Such schemes of breakdown prevention have been practiced in our airline and space industry for some time. In many cases, these prevention schemes have involved a greater knowledge of factors in production runs and production experience than is often found in the majority of industries. These protection schemes have been born out of the necessity of saving human life. The preventative schemes to be developed in industry in the future will emphasize that the proverbial ounce of prevention is worth a pound of cure, and these controls that alert management ahead of time to take preventative steps will be of greater and greater significance.

The prevention of breakdowns or the improvement of quality will come about in three different ways. The first will be care in designing equipment of increasingly higher reliability of performance. This development will be an outgrowth of the "drive for reliability" theme of the space, aircraft, and automotive industries, carried further into the reliability of manufacturing of many types of equipment. The second area of emphasis will be in the installation of further feedback and control mechanisms that will make certain processes self-regulating and certain types of errors self-correcting. The adjustment for size control and the adjustment for straightness of feed will be areas in which feedback control is feasible. The third area is related to the installation of fencing devices and warning mechanisms, whether they be electronic, hydraulic, or mechanical, that will give advance indication of corrective action required on the part of the operator, *before* rather than *after* the process has been shut down.

In all these areas, the trend will be toward a higher degree of utilization of expensive manufacturing processes and facilities. An important byproduct of this type of control will be higher yield and less waste in manufacturing. In many processes today, high material costs have made problems of yield more important than the cost of the labor of tending the equipment.

3. A Reduction of Line and an Increase in Staff Management

We have already described some of the reasons why we believe that there will be a substantial reduction of the middle-management line executive group, for the span of control of each line executive can be greater when he is serviced by the better information and physical control systems that have been discussed. The line job will be primarily that of monitoring and controlling the performance of expensive manufacturing processes and the direction of efforts to keep these processes producing high-quality goods on schedule. To say that the line job will be "merely monitoring" is to do injustice to that ingenuity and knowledge that key line people can add to the total situation. However, line executives will not be concerned in implementing innovations and control on a day-to-day basis. Rather, their observations will stimulate staff studies for intermediate-range planning, whereby processes, control, and information can be improved to maximize operating performance. Line management will have a greater appreciation of the skills and abilities needed to do the job rather than undertake this work itself.

The middle-management staff group, however, will find it necessary to have increasing competence in analytical ability, an understanding of all the functions of the business, and an appreciation for the use and manipulation of computer support facilities. The training requirements for this middle-management staff group will be more extensive than those required for the middle-management line group. It is always a greater task to equip oneself in the art of being able to perform, rather than in the art of being able to appreciate.

Some companies believe that the operations-research approach to industrial programs requires substantially more sophisticated information than actually may be desirable to solve worthwhile problems. It appears to us that the business and physical restrictions are controlling factors in most cases; understanding and proper handling of these makes the solution more satisfactory than mere sophistication in the approach. Consequently, even at the outset, many programs may require less operations-research per se and a better definition of the true restrictions of the process.

A second important function for operations research is to communicate and describe optimization techniques and logic to line and staff executives, so that there is a greater recognition of what is really being accomplished within the business and physical control system. The reluctance of many operations-research people to describe, in layman's language, the tools and skills of their trade has made them far less effective in business than they should be. Obviously, many operations researchers are not, by their nature, good communicators. Therefore, it is essential that the manager of operations research and at least some of his supporting personnel be good communicators with line and staff personnel who are not trained in the tools and techniques of optimization.

There appears to be little question that the number of middle and lower management personnel per dollar of sales will decrease, and the demands on those that remain will be more professional than they are presently. Staff work is likely to change from analysis of some data, with a lot of judgment, to the review of summary reports and simulations of major portions of the operations. From this review, staff will perform the synthesis necessary to recommend overriding the programmed response to get the best course of action under the particular circumstances.

Whether the old or the new type of staff work is more interesting is, perhaps, academic. Certainly, those that did staff work in the past and found out things that were valuable to management made a contribution that improved performance of their companies. The staff people of the future should find an equal amount of challenge in the analytical work because of the depth of penetration required in their studies.

It is difficult to forecast the magnitude of results. In some cases in the past a little bit of staff work may have accomplished substantial savings only because the opportunities were so great. In certain situations in the future, simulations of a situation may indicate that the improvement in certain areas is barely profitable. This is no criticism of the analyst. It may be that the margin for improvement is very shallow based upon the plateau of operations that has been achieved. It is here that the intuitive brilliance of staff work will make a substantial difference to the success of one company in comparison to another. Information and physical control processes will aid in bringing operations to the optimum point, but there is always the risk that only by breaking away and making a radical change in either the physical process or the control methods can substantial gains be achieved. (This is the old statistical concern—that we may have reached the top of the wrong mountain.) In some areas it will be possible, with the aid of simulations, to test many avenues without actually investing and trying on an actual fact basis. Where this is possible, the direction of staff efforts will be substantially more controlled and better directed than they have been in the past.

Although management should concentrate on the future in its planning and training, we see, unfortunately, that too much of today's planning is in the area of new products and new prophesies and not enough in the area of training to use new business systems merged with new physical control systems. We see management looking at the good results that have been achieved in a few instances where there has been adequate training, and contrasting this to the often more numerous circumstances where failures have developed because of inadequate training and support. It is going to require the training of line and staff personnel to understand and work effectively with the type of integrated information and physical control systems that we have described.

4.   Five Key Trends Moving into the 1980's*

I have chosen five very important trends in Manufacturing Data Systems that will be in the limelight from now through the early 1980's. These are:

- Material Requirements Planning systems moving from gross to net-change pegged requirements;
- Shop-floor control moving from data collection to on-line data control;
- Distributed data bases using Minicomputers;
- Paperless distribution, MRP, and shop-floor control systems;
- Management development for successful computer systems in industry.

These may not include all of the important trends—particularly for a few out-front companies, who are moving toward completely automated factories. In the number of companies, however, the job shops far exceed these, and it is toward this group that this paper is directed.

---

*From a paper presented to an AIIE-Systems Seminar in Chicago on Sept. 29, 76, by Arnold Putnam.

Trend 1 Material Requirements Planning Systems Moving
*from Gross to Net-Change Pegged Requirements**

The APIC's crusade for Materials Requirements Planning (MRP) has resulted in most companies having or developing an MRP system. Unfortunately, most of these are of the regeneration type, which requires a monthly or semimonthly re-explosion of the entire product structure.

The primary reason was that IBM's application approach led many of their clients in this direction.

When IBM released its PICS system in the late 1960's for the 360's, the more advanced industrial users considered it a step backward from the initial steps already taken supporting the Bill Processors for the 1440's and 1401's. Unfortunately, the original IBM personnel had been promoted or moved on and the PICS system was tied *to complete re-explosion with netting as separate and not built into the process.*

Many companies convinced themselves that starting MRP with Regeneration was a logical step and that the Net-Change Pegged Requirements feature could be added later. These companies now find that this step will require a major overhaul. Nevertheless, the 70 percent or better who can perform better with Net Change Pegged Requirements systems will be involved with this change from now through the early 1980's. The gains to be achieved are:

- Daily adjustment of work-order and purchasing priorities for the close-in needs of assembly or repair parts so that expediting and related costs can be eliminated.

- Less processing if the number of parts that have activity each day is relatively small.

- The confidence in a system tied to accurately portraying daily needs leads to substantial reduction in work-in-process inventory.

- Significant improvement in assembly efficiency related to almost perfect performance in the supply parts on schedule.

The exceptional performance of a few companies will provide the stimulus and the catalyst for the acceptance of Net Change Pegged MRP systems.

How will these companies implement this change? Many more will purchase complete or partial MRP Application Packages rather than to proceed with in-house development. There are an increasing number of these Application Packages available and they need careful examination in terms of:

- Quality
- Applicability

---

*See Appendix 2—Nordberg Case Study

- Flexibility
- Cost
- Consulting support

The purchaser is wise to have a team of both systems and user personnel visit a "going" application in making the selection ("all that glitters is not gold").

Trend 2 Shop-Floor Control Moving from
*   Data Collection to On-Line Control*

Many of the companies who installed data collection in the late '60's and '70's were disappointed with the failure to improve accuracy and to reduce costs. The hardware at the time was capable of delivering the input to the central station but offered little or no data editing or quick feedback of errors. Those companies that launched data accuracy programs before proceeding with data collection fared much better and removed the key-punching bottlenecks as well as speeding up the feedback cycle. There were a few misguided souls who wanted to make these early systems interactive and failed to realize that, in most shops, the next jobs had to be predicted several hours ahead in order to get the tools ready. The cost of running priority programs or updating MRP status in response to interactive signals was also ignored. (Some of the computer manufacturers have been guided by the profits of high core and storage devices and not by the cost effectiveness of the applications that they recommend.)

Today's terminal devices, however, offer a major step forward in shop-floor control systems. These are:

- The ability to edit check on the CRT and get immediate feedback.
- The ability to deal only with the truly variable input (i.e., pieces, time worked, etc.).
- The ability to advance jobs in the stream and recall priority lists.
- The reduction in shop paperwork and printouts, particularly stock status reports and work-center queue lists.
- Fast and accurate location of any order in process.
- The calculation of labor performance against standard and flashback on CRT terminal. (One of the complaints of the early data-collection systems was the loss of data for calculation of performance and the foremen believed they lost control in having to wait for the printouts on the next day.)
- Reduced reprocessing of daily error situations that are excessive in many existing data-collection systems.

All of these benefits are available through greater multichannel control devices and CRT's. In most cases the main route sheet (job progress) and inventory files are only updated on-line, but the main logistical programs (MRP, order release, and shop-priority update) are still run on a daily batch basis.

Probably less than 5 percent of American industry has converted to CRT's for shop data control, but this will accelerate in the late 1970's and should see completion in the early 1980's. Even though these devices and supporting systems make accuracy improvement easier, we have found that well-designed, participative training programs are worthwhile and capable of raising data accuracy from the fifty-eighty percent range into the high nineties.

Trend 3 Distributed Data Bases Using Minicomputers

The development of minicomputers at very low costs coupled with cheaper multichannel entry into main frames has provided industry with much greater flexibility. This flexibility will give the functional users both better service and control over their specific needs. There is some concern over the cost of the redundancy in data that would be stored in both the minis and in the central file. However, with the low cost of minis this may not be too much extra. One of the biggest complaints of existing centralized systems is the slow and costly problem of changing existing programs and installing new ones. This freedom has to be tempered to fit mainstream control requirements at every point of interface. This freedom does worry EDP managers (with some justification) that the minicomputer programs may not properly interface with the central computer in terms of operating systems or data-base control and that even the unrelated poor performance may indirectly reflect upon them as the EDP experts.

Some of the more astute EDP managers believe that there is a cost/effectivity decision to be made by segmenting some core and storage on large systems and dedicating them to a functional user. In effect saying, "Here is your mini—you can buy it cheaper from us than as a semi-independent system." This logic will not be as convincing in more remote locations because of the daytime long-lines transmission costs. While I believe the partitioned central computer will be cheaper in many cases, the "apparent independence" of the mini will be attractive to many functional users.

The major application areas for minis in Manufacturing Control Systems from now into the 1980's are:

a) ORDER ENTRY, STOCK AVAILABILITY INQUIRY, APPROPRIATE ACTION:
    whether centralized or decentralized at a number of Distribution Centers.

Some companies already use CRT's for most oi tnis function. However, minis add a more complete capability in the remote situation as well as in the ones requiring hard-copy output. An example—a midwestern household goods company can:

- Receive the customer order at the Eastern Branch, check the mini (updated from central the prior evening) for customer credit, and

- Print the order based upon the input of Customer I.D. Number and quantity and item numbers, thus providing more accurate descriptions, pricing, addressing, and totaling at lower costs.

- Check available inventory and separate the back-ordered items immediately to save reprocessing.

- Assign bin numbers to picking slips.

- Handle unfilled demand properly in order to make proper forecast predictions.

b) SHOP-FLOOR CONTROL AND PERFORMANCE CALCULATION

The mini not only offers the opportunities of receiving data on operation completions, calculating operator performance, and updating the Q-lists as shown available through the CRT terminals previously described, but it offers core and storage support and printing capability usually not found with CRT's. The core and storage combination make it possible to:

- Do priority resequencing and make easier the recall of alternative routings.

- Provide more complete data on performance calculations, summary on all personnel as the workday progresses.

c) IMPROVED REMOTE STOCK-STATUS CONTROL

Minis offer the opportunity for the users in materials control and receiving to be very close to the issues, receipts, parts due, and status within their responsibility. With proper programming, the batch updating of the master files can be handled very economically, with the redundant storage costs becoming the only extra charge for the flexibility of the mini. Bin records and location indexes can be eliminated with the information recalled on CRT.

d) INDUSTRIAL ENGINEERING NEEDS FOR OPERATION-SHEET PREPARATION AND CALCULATION

A few companies have recognized the huge data-processing requirement in the work-standards area and have developed computerized Standard Data Programs. The current effectiveness of these programs is limited to the ease and accuracy of standards maintenance for changes either in data elements or in methods or equipment.

With mini computers to store and make prior data available and with group-technology code numbers for cross reference, a significant improvement can be made in the cost of preparing new operation sheets.

Thus a part similar to another—except for an additional or longer machining operation—can be recalled and the adjustment made for the difference without destroying the original and the new operation sheet prepared by changing only 5 to 10 percent of the data. Such operation sheets are more consistent in method and standard than having each new part number methodized from scratch frequently by a different person.

The average number of operations per part usually exceeds six; consequently the ultimate operation sheet file may exceed the routing or part master by a six-to-one ratio.

• Design engineering groups may want a mini for recall of similar-to parts and bills of material in preparing new and revised products.

Trend 4   Paperless Distribution, MRP, and Shop-Floor Control Systems

This item could have been incorporated into Trend 3, but I have chosen to make a distinction in order to emphasize a far-reaching concept that could be easily ignored by the less imaginative or daring managers. We have heard quite a lot of talk of a paperless purchase, credit card, and banking systems. We have not heard enough about the paperless operation of industry.

It will be possible—by adding an output device to the mini station—to:

• Eliminate much of the shop-order and distribution-order paperwork.
• Print throw-away instructions for the operator.
• Have all other data printed only on request.
• Eliminate many inventory and warehouse status reports.

The work order would need only a number tag with the lot; all other instructions and reference material would be on the CRT backed up by the mini for:

• Job move instructions
• Queue Lists and Work Order Number Priority
• Formats for receiving input data on:

a) Job moves;
b) Pieces produced, time used, operator identification;
c) Job completions;
d) Queue list deletions and additions;

e) Performance calculations;

f) Employee performance accumulations;

g) Scrap, reason code, responsibility formats;

h) Rework, instructions and charges.

One could argue that the throw-away operator instruction sheet could be abandoned, but the chance of error in moving to the machine, doing the job, and properly encoding the transaction at the end would not be worth the risk.

Trend 5 Management Development for Successful Industry Computer Systems*

I believe the advent of distributed data·bases using minicomputers is going to accentuate the need for EDP-user understanding and successful interface. Where this does not develop, the minis will probably become mostly independent. The users may be satisfied with half a loaf because they will never properly perceive what the full loaf would be like. In these companies the central computer will more and more be used for the accounting and historical record-keeping systems. Such a development means that users will not get the benefits of the high-core daily batch programs such as Daily Net Change MRP and the resulting change in the priorities of shop orders. It will mean that logistics will be piecemeal and not what's best for the company as a whole from forecast and master schedule through shop responses.

We have made substantial progress in EDP-user understanding.

Summary

In selecting and outlining these key trends, I have had a high degree of confidence. Most trends follow unsatisfied needs and these all fit into that category.

In predicting the effectiveness of industrial companies in dealing with these trends, I have far less confidence. There has been a basic dilemma in the effective development up to the present time, created by the conflict between:

● The chief executive's desire to let each key executive run his own show and to hold him accountable

and

● the need for every functional executive to support long-range Management Information Systems development and to properly interface on this with both EDP and all other functions.

---

*See Appendix 1—Mapping of a Purchasing, Production and Inventory Control operation.

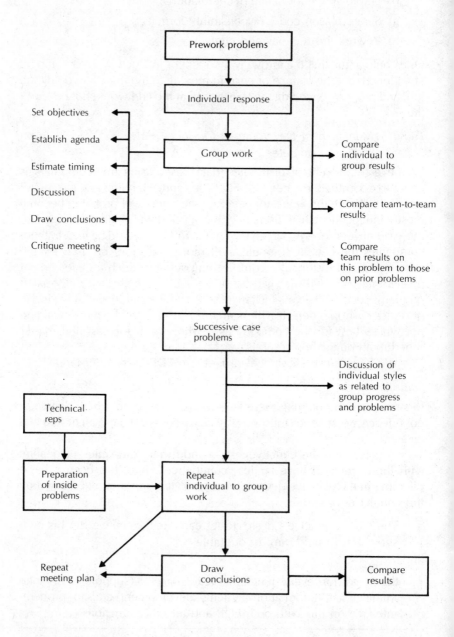

Figure 7.1

Unfortunately, the advent of the low-cost mini seems to permit the chief executive to let each function go its own way and to pay less attention to EDP and interfunction cooperation. In my opinion, the ultimate effectiveness of manufacturing and all other management information systems in the 1980's rests with the hope of enlightenment of the chief executive on this point. Will we have "half a loaf" of what is available, or be with the best and get the "whole thing?"

5. Merger of Physical Control of Operations with Integrated Information-Control Systems

a)   Integrated Information-Control System in Operation

In a previous text entitled *Unified Operations Management,** the integrated information and control system was described as one that started from forecasting and order entry, and proceeded through to the distribution and sale of the final product, with control of all of the mainstream activities in between. Recent advances in data-communications equipment indicate that there would be a real advantage in many industries in tying major customers into the information network. Such a step could provide both operating economy and rapid service to the market. In some situations individual companies already have stolen a jump on their competitors by providing inexpensive data-transmission systems and basic information for their distributors and major customers. Their customers are now able to place their orders upon the source of supply far more rapidly and accurately, and to reduce their accounts payable and receiving transactions through the use of the prepunched or precoded information that has been made available in these circumstances. These same advanced companies are finding that the stimulation of their suppliers to provide them with data-transmission and collection facilities and prepunched information permits them to make savings in their purchasing operations and in their accounts payable by the use of much recaptured nonvariable data.

The salesmen in competitive companies obviously face a disadvantage when they are trying to sell against a system of supply that is faster and more accurate in terms of customer service than the type of operation that they are still required to provide. In the long run, where cost and quality are nearly equal, the supplier that offers the greatest convenience of service enhances his position.

Those who have visited new equipment shows have observed equipment, machines, and processes that were capable of automatic controls in terms of feeding the process, producing the goods, and supplying them to the users. Such a method of operation is obviously

*Unified Operations Management, McGraw Hill 1963 Putnam A.O., Barlow E.R. and Stilian, G. Revised by Rath & Strong 1969

easier to establish in certain types of industries than in those that have the complexity of job-shop operations. The problem of company size also has a relationship to the cost and payback of making progress in the total information and control systems area. Some of the smaller companies may find it possible to obtain the competitive advantages of many of the techniques and concepts described in this book by the use of service bureaus, or computer facilities shared with other smaller companies in their immediate vicinity. Where this is ruled out, the operating advantages enjoyed by companies that can support physical control of processes integrated with the information-control operations may force these smaller companies to combine, in order to maintain and improve their competitive positions.

In an optimum operation the predominant amount of information is pregenerated from prepunched or prepared data files, and is transmitted throughout the information system, with a minimum amount of hard copy produced for documentation purposes. The system should provide the ability to summarize in terms of hard copy, or to print out information about specific things upon inquiry from interested parties. With this type of operation, management-by-exception will be developed to a realistic degree, and the computer control system will provide the power to watch a multitude of activities but to report only on those that go beyond control limits.

In certain types of industry, it may be feasible to start the manufacturing processes immediately upon command from the information and control system in a type of pushbutton plant; this degree of automation may be less easily adapted to the types of industry where it is necessary to have queue lines of work awaiting various manufacturing processes, to fill the hills and valleys that are characteristic of these systems. Obviously, in converting certain types of chemicals or in batch manufacturing processes, it would be more feasible to switch immediately to different types of mixes and grades from raw material supplies that are already available upon command of the computer. In job-shop types of operations, there may have to be a storage of buffer jobs waiting to go into manufacturing upon command from the information and control system. It should be possible, however, to rerank the jobs that are awaiting manufacture in the buffer or queue list by changes in priority that take place within the information and control system before any particular job is actually committed to physical manufacturing. In certain industries, moreover, the physical manufacturing process can continue under computer and material-handling control untouched by human hands. In the foreseeable future, it is more difficult to visualize the conventional machining or fabricating type of operation with this kind of control. It is more likely that each individual machine or group of machines will be under some type of computer tape or numerical control system, which will minimize the setup and the actual piece handling in and out of the machine. The efficiency in making these tapes and in sequencing the job may be much affected by group technology and coding systems, as previously discussed. It may be necessary, however, to use conveyors or other types of linkages to pass the semifinished parts from one operation to another. The degree of automation of physical handling between operations should be determined by a cost-and-savings study in each case. Much can be done in terms of combining similar types of products and parts into family groups, so that the convenience of dealing with a job-shop type of operation upon a semimass-production basis becomes far more feasible than if the size and configuration are allowed to change completely at random as the orders are released to the physical manufacturing operations.

In summary, the look ahead into the late 1970's and early 1980's visualizes a rapid development of integrated information and control systems, from the area of forecasting and order entry through the areas of materials requirements, procurement, production scheduling, distribution, and accounting control. This type of integrated information system will have the basic logic in terms of when and how much to order from suppliers and from its own manufacturing facilities, and when and how much to ship to customers and points of distribution within its command. Increasing amounts of attention will be given to the numerical or computer control of complex manufacturing processes where substantial amounts of direct labor have been expended in setting up this type of operation in the past. These physical manufacturing processes will be monitored by feedback mechanisms that will control yield and quality. size, and various other types of physical phenomenon. The ultimate linkage of the physical and the managerial control systems will take place with varying degrees of speed, depending upon the logic and complexity of these two systems in each type of industry. It appears extremely important that the faster a particular industry goes toward an integrated information and physical manufacturing control system, the more pressing the problem of training new managers and new operating people at all levels becomes.

b) Substantial Reductions in Direct Labor

During the past thirty years there has been considerable cause for concern about the reduction in the labor force due to the mechanization of many manufacturing processes. It is quite true that these manufacturing mechanizations have reduced the unit labor hours by substantial amounts in almost every type of industry. At the same time, greater and greater facilities have developed to meet the worldwide demands of other industries and the consumer market. The very factors that have provided improved mechanization have also brought about the employment of labor and capital to produce the improved facilities. What was true of mechanization during this period is also true of the automation being experienced at the present time, both in the field of managerial and physical manufacturing processes. The requirements in terms of capital and manpower to build the automatic control devices in automatic control systems is substantial, and the increasing worldwide markets are placing demands upon our labor force to meet the expanding usage of goods and facilities. Consequently, in many situations it may well be that the reductions in direct labor are offset by transplanting this direct labor to new types of jobs in new companies. It is important, however, that company managers be aware of the fact that the retraining of direct labor may be necessary to fit these individuals into the new scheme of events and operations. The type of direct labor involved in the setting up of manufacturing processes and the adjustment of these processes to produce goods, parts, and services may be gradually eliminated by computer control, which can set up and adjust these production facilities more rapidly and more accurately than the labor force has been able to do in the past. However, there will have to be an increase in the type of labor necessary to monitor and to service operations in this new computer control age. So there will be, on one hand, a reduction in the direct labor force and a change in its complexity because a portion of it will have to have even greater technical capabilities to service the complex machinery that is being produced today; and, on the other hand, there will be another portion of a labor force that will provide more routine monitoring type of control, which will be needed to see that these operations are being carried out successfully and to push buttons when difficulties are encountered.

c)   Substantial Reductions in Clerical Force

A substantial reduction in the clerical force will be the result of the automation of clerical and information-control operations.

Up to the present the impact of computer control has largely been offset by the expansion of American industry to serve the worldwide demands placed upon it. Most of the automation has been strictly in clerical functions of the business, and there has been little impact of the complete automation of an integrated information and control system. In the few companies where the latter has been accomplished, the performance has not been sufficiently perfected to the degree that managers feel confident about operating their total system with little duplicate effort on the part of the clerical and indirect staff. There is little doubt, however, that competitive pressures and the improved excellence of the operation of the total control systems will have a far greater impact in the future than anything that has happened until now, in terms of the displacement of clerical and indirect people in our industrial operations. Opportunities will exist for some of these people in the numerous data-preparation jobs that will be continually generated by the demands of these new systems. Other opportunities will be possible in the operation of the computer equipment and in the programming of the systems that will carry out the management information and control technology. There is a question as to whether the openings for these new types of skills will be sufficient to absorb those freed up. There is steady progress towards "paperless" manufacturing systems which will use CRT (Cathode Ray Terminals) and MINI computers with all the available stored data ready for recall. This will eliminate many outputs and status reports. Consideration of the number of people engaged in sales record-keeping, requirements planning, inventory posting, job location and expediting, traffic distribution, and accounting, and the fact that a large portion of this posting operation will be accomplished within the information and control system, will give a reasonable measure of the magnitude of the problem to be faced in this area. It may well be that some opportunities will be created for skills of this type in the direct labor operations of the monitoring of computer controls.

B. THE NEW LABOR FORCE

1. Composition

Parallel to the reduction of the manpower needed to set up and operate industrial equipment, an increase of trained electronic and mechanical maintenance personnel can be anticipated. The use of computers for both information and process control will progress at an ever-increasing pace, but computers will require continual and rapid maintenance service. This is not because the equipment fails to operate with a high degree of perfection; rather it is a result of the requirement for perfection demanded under the new *modus operandi*. The old segmented, slow, bit-by-bit processing of control data and physical production required substantial amounts of float or buffer work between each step. Consequently, with the failure of process, those downstream operated on float while the repair was being carried out. In our new world of integrated real-time operations, the control and physical systems operate rapidly and completely. Mechanical or electronic failures in one area may stop the whole process; a missing item of control data may do the same. To those who conclude that this concept will fail because of these restrictions, one can only comment that complex weapons and missile systems currently operate with this reliability and accuracy, as do many separated information and physical control systems.

In almost all information or physical control processes, competent programming can aid in the evaluation of the failure. Even with this aid, however, the final analysis and correction of difficulties will require skilled personnel and quick service, because of the financial and operating impact of serious delays.

The mechanical and hydraulic operations of physical production facilities are also becoming more complicated, and, in some cases, the problems may lie in interaction with the computer control mechanisms. Some of these facilities can be operated with manual override while the difficulties are being overcome; in other cases this will be impossible.

While the number of personnel with general electro-mechanical training will continually increase, the supply will not be great enough to cover the demand. Training in a specific type of computer and manufacturing equipment will fall almost 100 percent upon industry. The task in larger companies will not appear as threatening, as they have had in-house capabilities upon which they can expand. Medium-sized and smaller companies will have to develop some facilities or form coopera-tive training ventures to fill the need.

An appraisal of the range of good to bad performance in a number of companies at the present time shows that the magnitude of the problem and its effect is not fully appreciated by most managements because they lack good norms upon which to pass judgement, and they accept substandard performance as adequate.

2.   Increase in Human Monitoring of the Automatic Process

While the need to set up and adjust equipment will be seriously reduced, as mentioned previously, the number of personnel monitoring operations will increase. The span of control of the people in this phase of activity will be larger than that existing today, and the jobs will be aided by sensing devices, kick-off switches, feedback corrections, and the like. There are some situations in which manual override or action ahead of a shutdown may save the time and cost of permitting the automatic devices to act. For example, twisted material or a defect may hit a sensing device and stop the process, but if it had been straightened out while in motion, shutdown and startup losses would not have occurred. The monitoring job will have to be dealt with effectively, though there is some indication that people can carry out this type of work with a minimum of concentration. It is not unlike that of the special traffic policeman on construction jobs, who merely permits the expensive equipment to keep on rolling while the public waits. Years ago when road work was largely manual, the ratio of traffic policemen to people employed was undoubtedly much lower than it is today.

3. Increase in Data-Processing and Systems Personnel

At the outset of many complex systems it appears that there is almost a complete reassignment of the direct, indirect, and clerical personnel displaced. Obviously, after installation the turnover ratio changes to one more favorable to the new investment. Nevertheless, the demand for data-processing and systems personnel is already greater than the supply, and this situation may get progressively worse. Fortunately, this activity offers a creative challenge to many who might otherwise find routine monitoring work dull in the new computer world. These people must have high mathematical and reasoning aptitudes to perform satisfactorily. Senior systems work will require the equivalent of college or advanced degrees. Much of the selection and training of this staff will have to be carried on in the plant. Considering a three- to five-year time span for developing senior systems people, many companies are already behind the eightball, and their current and future computer programs will suffer substantially as a consequence.

It is difficult to evaluate the impact of the lack of skills on efficiency in the area of programming and systems design. The responsibility for investing sufficiently in the training and development of people who can produce competent work in this area lies with managerial personnel in the system departments. The more professional we become about the operation of all phases of the EDP department, the higher the skill requirement will go. More rigorous training will result in lower total manpower needs.

There is some long-run possibility that the continued development of successful application packages for accounting and operational areas may reduce the demand for systems designers and programmers. While this decline is occurring, it will be offset by the expansion of demands in the MIS–Physical Operations area. In a similar way, keypunching may be reduced by better input devices and turnaround data, but the total demand may continue to rise because of the expansion in the whole field of computer operations.

C. MIS RESPONSIBILITY*

This will change in the future. MIS, now solidly a staff function, will become an internal service/consulting group. Small and highly specialized, their major task will be to consult to users throughout the company on:

---

*MIS (as described here) does not include the operation of EDP, which may or may not be a separate function.

- User needs leading to system design and redesign;
- Training users to understand and use systems designed for them;
- Training users to train new employees.

The MIS staff member of the future, then, will be expert at systems and also will understand human behavior, group interaction and dynamics, behavioral-science training techniques, and techniques of data gathering and needs assessment.

D. THE NEW MIDDLE MANAGEMENT

1. Front-Line Management

The foreman often has been called the front line of management. In some companies he is regarded as spokesman for labor. Most foremen believe that they really are in "no man's land." A fair amount has been said about automation forcing foremen out of jobs, in a similar manner to what mechanization in the past two decades has done to people in the labor force. It appears true that the foreman's job is being and will continue to be drastically affected, and that fewer numbers of foremen will be required for equivalent volumes of production. If the total national production continues to rise, however, the foreman will find new opportunities, just as labor has, during mechanization.

Some probable changes in requirements for the foreman's position are listed in Table 7.1.

The middle management group is typically made up of superintendent, staff department heads, and assistant function or line managers. In considering the impact of computer-based information and control systems, middle management can be considered in part as a group, and in part each area must be discussed separately. The general situation will be dealt with first.

2. More Responsibility for Equipment and Less for Personnel

While managers can never overlook the personnel aspects of their job, the balance is certain to shift in the direction of more concern for the capital investment under each executive. The planning for, the acquisition, installation, operation, and maintenance of these facilities are going to require an increasing amount of attention.

Our high proportion of continuous-process type of industries have had this high investment problem for some time; so the management here will only notice an increased emphasis on these factors. The semimass-production and job shop operations, however, generally have not been exposed to this type of situation. Their thinking is geared to a one- or two-shift operation of the assets at the most. Standby equipment,

Table 7.1   Requirements for Foreman's Position.

Former Activities	Effect of New Requirements
1. Scheduling of Work	Decreased
2. Assignments	Decreased
3. Assisting with process setup	Decreased
4. Issue of tools and equipment	Decreased
5. Inspection	Increased
6. Performance review	Decreased
7. Supervising	Increased
8. Training	Increased

inventory between stations, and the use of depreciated facilities have led to less careful planning and a primary concern for the labor cost. The middle management group will be more concerned with high throughputs of good quality products at low maintenance costs.

The middle-management staff group of the future will have a greater responsibility for the large capital investment in complex automated equipment. The uptime of this equipment will be the major concern of the line executive. In most cases standby equipment will be available only when multi-units are involved and a small number is kept in reserve. This will place a premium on corrective action for difficulties and preventative maintenance.

The line executive will be primarily concerned with yield, while the quality control and manufacturing engineer group investigate changes and adjustments that will eliminate potential trouble spots. The staff requirements for technical studies in both the physical and information process will be high and require the training now provided only in exceptional companies.

3.   Greater Understanding of Complete Process and Interrelationships

In the past most staff work has been within a function (sales, manufacturing, engineering, finance) of the business. With the development of integrated information and control systems, the creation of the central staff appears almost axiomatic. (See *Unified Operations Management,* pp. 72–84.) With the further step of linking the information system with process control, the central staff will be a must. Whether a small resident staff should be left in each function or these would be served better by a single central staff is questionable. Certainly, there is likely to be some staff resident within the functions during the transition period.

What will the central staff do? In the field of inventory control and materials management, they will consider the course of action from forecast to distribution, developing the best integrated plan for the entire company.

In the area of quality control, the problems will be evaluated from customer, engineering, and manufacturing viewpoints.

In the financial area, the optimum course will be determined in the alternate use of funds, the performance being measured in terms of both direct responsibility and corporate accountability.

E.   THE NEW STAFF MANAGEMENT

The percentage of staff in management and the quality of that staff are both going to increase. The impact on profits of staff recommendations will be more and more significant in the years ahead. While the line managers will need more indoctrination and training than they do now, the staff personnel has to keep even further ahead in the new hardware and software for both MIS and physical operations, including the ability to train the others.

1.   Greater Need for Staff Generalists

The role and training of the staff specialists will be covered in the next section. The more difficult job is to develop the generalists in the staff who comprehend the total picture, so that the plans will be neither unbalanced nor unrealistic.

There is an old adage that "good line men make poor staff and vice versa." This may apply to the majority, but there always has been a healthy minority who excel at both. The staff people generally have a higher intellectual level, which permits them to penetrate further into problems and to develop solutions. The line people usually are more action-oriented; they either have less intellectual capacity or do not care to exploit it. But the minority are those staff people who have excellent leadership potential and excel at it and the line officers capable of quick comprehension and penetration of complex staff work.

Out of this group, industry must cultivate the staff generalists, who will provide the broad direction of the staff and be the principal communication link with the line.

The practical broadening of the staff generalist will not happen by chance. Management must develop a training pattern that will keep producing sufficient candidates of this type on a continuing basis. This pattern should include some exposure to field and plant operations, probably through actual assignment. Following this, assignments as internal or external consultants on projects of major importance are desirable. Ample opportunity for continued education and idea-swapping at special courses or seminars should be provided during the entire period. It seems wise to consider more interchange between staff and line positions at higher levels.

2.   Need for More Technically Qualified Specialists

Staff specialists in the past have had deep involvement in their particular function. In most cases, these people knew little about the other operations of the business.

The computer is affecting this situation directly and indirectly. In every staff segment of the business, programs have been developed to automate previous work and to aid in a deeper and more sophisticated analysis. Indirectly, the computer has provided the means for the rapid development of integrated management information systems. The flow of data for information and control and the integration of reports makes it necessary for each function to become more knowledgeable about the other, in terms of both objectives and needs.

The training of staff specialists in computer techniques, software support, and programs is already being accomplished to a considerable degree in many companies. Where this is not being done, management either has failed to support such efforts with time and funds, or they do not have sufficiently competent personnel to take advantage of such efforts.

The training of staff personnel in the practicalities of the business operation as well as in the operations and needs in other functional areas is being accomplished only by a few of the larger and more advanced companies. These generally have resorted to a three- to six-months' course given away from the job. In rare cases, such courses are also backed up by actual assignments in the other areas. It seems advisable to explore a part-time, continuing exposure that increases the discourse between the staff specialists in each area. Perhaps two to three hours a week in either work time or evening sessions would accomplish more than the programs based upon complete removal from the scene. In the long run, both of these methods will play an important role in the cross-training that is required.

F.   NEW TOP MANAGEMENT IN THE COMPUTER AGE

1.   Functional Managers' Responsibility for Performance

A chief executive, frustrated after months of interviewing prospective divisional managers, remarked, "I believe it's a lot more difficult to find good industrial captains than it is admirals. An admiral has to lead and judge the competence of several key executives; the captain has to know a hell of a lot of detail about running the ship."

This may bave been true in the past; it may be an erroneous assumption in the computer age. To assume that the chief executive can evaluate the rate of investment, the competence of the divisional executive, the performance of the divisions and functions in this new age without a real appreciation of how the operations are carried out, may have substantial risks. Many industries, including more than one computer manufacturer, have been experiencing trouble with inadequate plans and continuous follow-through during the recent years of rapid change.

There are industries in which the impact will be felt far ahead of others, but, eventually, it will be true in all: the new chief executives must come from a field of new divisional captains. Present chief executives should be concerned with training enough potential leaders and exposing them to these new challenges and modes of operation so that the future is not limited by the backgrounds and capabilities of their successors. Unless this is done, except for the small percentage of younger admirals who are willing to be retrained and reoriented, there will probably be a turning to more youthful presidents (who have not been captains long) and a shelving of some of today's chief executives who are too strongly related to the old rules. This may parallel the reaching down to the younger, more vigorous, more recently trained men in selecting many of our key leaders during World War II.

The key point is that effective operation in the computer age requires a change in divisional and functional relationships that can be accomplished only if understood and directed from the top. The interrelationship of the planning, logistics, and information-flow demands coordination, attention, and compromise for effective implementation. This, in turn, can be accomplished only by an admiral who understands the new rules by which the captains run their business.

As we observe management's attempts (in a variety of industries) to deal with the transition to computer-based information and control systems, we are astounded at the wide range of results. In some companies the transition has been carried out with a high degree of success, while in others it has been fraught with difficulty. In the former cases, the results may have made the difference between profit and loss or substantial improvements in profits; while in the latter, the results may have been inconsequential or have created actual losses. While it is accurate to say that the support of top management is the key factor in explaining the difference, such a statement is a misleading oversimplification of the situation. Top management, but frequently only the chief executives, set the real goals and the pace of change in many companies. Thus, if the profit goal is twice as high in Company A without computer-based information systems, as is the goal in B *with* one, A is still likely to "out-earn" B. On the other hand, when A teams up with a sound information and control system, the results will exceed the previous profits of either firm.

The chief executive usually works with only seven to ten people directly, but his establishment of targets and insistence on results sets the tone for the entire organization. We are all aware of the impact that a single man has in changing a poor profit situation into a good one. There are times when running an industry is like a naval engagement. When a sub, already slightly damaged, is caught on the surface by an enemy cruiser, it may mean death to go below, but it is suicide to stay on the surface. However, when the sub captain finds that he can survive beneath, he may not attack. In parallel, many businesses that have made drastic reductions to create profits may not take the next step and expend funds for long-term growth and sound development. Many business leaders feel that all of the subordinates have to be treated with approximately equal budgetary changes; more competent ones recognize that the more efficient areas should not be curtailed as much as the inefficient ones. More important, these latter managers recognize that there are only a few areas where added expenditures will create substantial returns and that substantial added investment should be made in these areas while holding the other functions in line or even decreasing them. To maintain motivation and coordination when on such a course takes real leadership. In most companies the development of integrated information and control systems is one of these areas, and support by the chief executive will pay high dividends in the years to come.

2. Plan Simulation for the Company as a Whole

An increasing number of programs are being used for long-range strategy on products, growth, and facilities, based upon discounted return on investment or assets-employed calculations. Most of these elements are made on data from all functions resulting in company-wide projections, with some of the programs run at various probability levels.

The number and location of plants and warehouses is typical of this type of analysis. The recommendations thus become more of a "total" decision than functional alone. In the past, manufacturing decided where to put the plants, and marketing decided where to put the branches and warehouses; top management primarily influenced the *timing*—usually by delaying (not advancing) the commitment of funds and/or personnel to support such a step. With a simulation based on total operations, top management is more likely to make the decision on both timing and specific action; however, such decisions should be made with the advice and counsel of all functions concerned. The danger here is that the problem may defy complete definition; and, unless caution prevails, top management may implement the right decision to the wrong situation. Competitive action is a case in point; the decision on plant and warehouse location for the next ten years may look great until the competitor selects a new site that is adjacent to an expanding portion of the market. Humans can raise the questions; computer programs cannot.

On the operational side (in contrast to longer-range strategic planning), the dynamic plan continually unfolds based upon the latest input information. Management has two responsibilities here:

a)   Does the strategy coded into the decision rules in the computer programs still appear appropriate for the actual performance in terms of sales, costs, etc.?

b)   Are there out-of-control situations that need immediate investigation and corrective action?

It will be difficult for the general executive to watch either of these closely, and success frequently may be related to the alert functional officers who move in time.

In consulting, we often contrast the range of capabilities in this regard by two expressions:

"He can smell where something is wrong by looking at the report."

"He wouldn't know it unless it hit him over the head."

3.   Top Line Officers with Staff Background

Because of the changing environment previously described in this chapter, we believe that an increasing number of top line officers will come from the staff rather than from the line, as has been customary in the past.

Manufacturing managers, who have frequently come from the superintendents' group, will now more likely be promoted from the industrial engineering, systems, materials, or quality-control areas.

Controllers, who have come from accounting areas, may now come from systems or industrial engineering. Sales managers, who usually come from top field salesmen, may more frequently come from marketing strategy areas.

Chief engineers, who frequently were the best inventors, may now come from those who best understand product families, building-block design concepts, and the like.

General executives are usually promoted from the level below, but if these people already have greater staff experience, then these skills will now be raised to a higher level.

The organizational importance and prestige of good functional performance must be continued. Equal pay for the best inventory controller or best salesman must be considered even though such positions may not lead to the top of the organization as often as they have in the past.

4.　Officer Accountability for Functional Override

There is a real danger of becoming systems and computer dependent. Dramatic cases such as the Northeast Blackout show this. The computer program probably will average nine times out of ten to have the best answer, but the tenth time may offset all of the rest. Management must reward those who successfully override the program recommendations and not unduly condemn those that override and come off second-best. There is logic for this, and management should maintain an environment that encourages human judgment. If an operator had cut off western New York during the power surge, he could have saved New York City and New England, a sure gain of 20 to 1. But not cutting off western New York, he ran the risk of saving 1 by gambling 20. The kid that felt the worst about it was the one "who kicked the pole" at the moment of failure and thought he carried the whole thing. Business, too, must worry about spurious correlations.

A man who overrides the sales forecast and orders extra stock may risk higher inventory, but the potential gain in profits may be much higher. Programs and statistics are very poor at abrupt changes; humans excel at quick recognition. Top management must encourage this override.

5.　More Complete Analysis of Competitors' and Industry's Actions

Some companies know as much about their major competitors as the insiders know. Usually, little is known about some others—even their share of certain markets in contrast to the total sales. Even less is known about competitive products, quantities sold, good and bad features. Without involvement in business espionage, a company can purchase, test, and analyze a competitor's products as well as pinpoint strengths and weaknesses.

Perhaps, the weakest link in information about competitors is lack of knowledge by which to estimate their probable course of action. There is nothing wrong with "putting one's self in the other guy's shoes" and evaluating his position in regard to finance, products, personnel, and facilities, in order to reason out his general course of action. An estimate of this may clarify the best course of action for one's own company and particularly the *time* of action for the campaign involved.

6.   Greater Involvement in Worldwide Markets, Problems, and Training

We are facing a future of reduced barriers to trade and faster and cheaper transportation and communication, which will increase competition in both ideas and costs. There will be an increasing number of alternatives to one's products, or alternatives in the use of funds. Conversely, the alert, oriented, and trained manager in most businesses will see this as a greater opportunity rather than a greater threat.

Such people will have to travel more, study more, and work harder, but the returns should be greater than the reduced scope offered in the past. Because of this, more people will study (or restudy) foreign languages; and more people will try to understand foreign customs and business methods.

G.   SUMMARY

This is a managerial book about Management Information Systems in manufacturing industries. The managerial concerns are both about directing the MIS system itself, and directing the overall business operations.

In the chapters on Design and Implementation, many of the case examples are from the production and inventory-control field. This is both because this area was more out of control during implementation and because the author has had more extensive experience in this area. However, most of the managerial points and some of the more technical ones are equally applicable to sales, distribution, and accounting subsystems as well.

This book should lead to the development of a management check list. It is easy to overlook some of these points when you are a professional; the busy manager is far more vulnerable. MIS systems are difficult enough if everything is going well; each additional problem reduces the chance of success.

Looking toward the future, managers should begin to deal with the computer applications in the physical production area as well.

To many managers this book may present too difficult a role in MIS systems—to the energetic leader it may open some doors, so he can do the management job more capably and more fully.

QUESTIONS

	Poor	Slow	Average	Good	Excellent	Superior
1. Are we training for new management requirements in a computerized operation?						
2. Are we prepared, in the computer and the physical plant, to overcome breakdowns and other serious interruptions?						
3. Are we sensitive to the shift from line to staff?						
4. Are we sensitive to the shift from operating to monitoring and controlling? Can we maintain interest and morale in this environment?						
5. In a more specialized world, are we training enough generalists, who may no longer just evolve from the aging process?						
6. Are our managers competent to deal with major shifts of direction suggested by simulation, models, etc.?						
7. Are we willing to commit to the ongoing training—and ongoing workshop processes—to keep current with technology and current in its acceptance into our management system?						

Mapping of a Purchasing, Production and Inventory-Control Operation

I. THE CONCEPTUAL FRAMEWORK

The conceptual framework for the OMD portion of the consultant diagnosis is made up of at least two discrete yet related and dependent parts. As a way to introduce these parts, it may be helpful if we provide a brief, overall introduction, then outline a description of each part of our framework.

INTRODUCTION

Any diagnosis and subsequent analysis is best thought of as a tool for decision-making, problem-solving, and planning; and, further, as a tool that must be represented in the management-skills "package" of any manager in today's society.

There are two implications for this opening statement. The first is that the ability to accurately diagnose complex situations and to glean from that diagnosis information necessary to make high-quality decisions is a *skill*. This, like any other skill, can be learned and can be improved upon.

Many years of empirical research and experience in the management sciences, in the behavioral sciences, and in Organization Development have indicated that, as our world becomes more and more complex, there is more and more information available that must be factored into decisions that we all make every minute of the day. Another result of this complexity is that we must be aware of the various ramifications (to others) of our decisions, because it is only on extremely rare occasions today that we make decisions that do not somehow affect other people. The result of this, of course, is that managers must be able to filter through information, to systematically consider effects of decisions, and be able to perform more quickly and more accurately than ever before. We believe the key to accomplishing this feat is a diagnostic skill.

The second implication is that a diagnosis is a tool that can be used to maximum effectiveness and can also be *misused*. It can be misused by a diagnostician who does not include the appropriate components; or who does not have the skills to effectively analyze and draw conclusions; or who receives output of a diagnosis and uses data to fulfill needs based on self-interest and not on what is best for all people involved. There is a note of caution, then, in the use of diagnostic tools; and there should be a sense of responsibility in those who are charged with both the implementation of a diagnosis and the use of its results.

Considering these two issues, a theoretical foundation has evolved that provides a sound basis for diagnosis and also can increase the likelihood of using diagnostic studies properly and achieving maximum benefits from the information they provide. A brief description of two tenets that make up this framework is provided below*

1. THE MANAGER AS DECISION-MAKER

A manager is a problem-solver and a decision-maker who is constantly under pressure to balance two sometimes conflicting needs. One need is to maximize the likelihood that his or her organization (whether it be a department or a corporation) will achieve desired results; the other is for that same organization to satisfy the needs of the people who make it up. The dilemma often faced by today's manager is what to do when one need is in obvious conflict with the other. Does one sacrifice the objectives of the organization because some of the needs of some of the people are not being met? At what point does the manager make a choice between the two? What are the manager's own priorities and how do they fit with each set of needs?

These are provocative questions that cannot be ignored. Some managers would prefer to somehow reduce the pressure created by such dichotomies and choose to reorganize in such a way as to force the organizational structure to solve the problem; here the manager takes care of results and the personnel staff takes care of people. The problem, of course, is that the course often merely intensifies the problem of the conflict rather than alleviating it. Responsibility for managing either results or people cannot be totally delegated and certainly cannot be abdicated.

There may be another answer to the dilemma, however. It may be embodied in the fact that the more accurate information one has, the better able one is to make decisions; further, the better able one is to anticipate and accurately perceive problem symptoms before they cause crises, the better able one is to solve problems and to control one's own destiny. At the core of this possible solution is accurate, timely diagnosis. If, for example, a manager can pinpoint the potential dilemma of organization goals versus people's needs, the better able he or she is to see that dilemma solved.

The points, then, of this tenet are (a) that managers have, by the nature of their position, a responsibility to their organization and to the people who make it up; (b) that information is needed constantly if managers are to be able to make high-quality decisions so that the needs of both the organization and its people can be met to the maximum amount possible; and (c) that diagnosis, completely and accurately done, is a necessary tool to enable managers to obtain such information.

---

*Some of the material below is taken from the work of Walter R. Mahler.

2. DATA AS A STIMULANT FOR CHANGE

A second basic tenet is that data is a necessary stimulant for individual as well as organizational change. The noted adult educator Malcolm Knowles contends (and his research seems to be borne out) that an individual will not change his behavior or attitudes toward others unless he perceives a strong need to do sò. Our assumption is that the same is true with organizations in their quest to change and improve. Such recognition is most likely to arise when the individual or the organization sees a striking gap between the current state of affairs and some desired or preferred state. Such a variance is best revealed through the use of data which highlight factors making up current situations and which display significant blocks to achievement of the desired end.

This tenet provides insight into diagnostic study methodology; i.e., having a set of goals and desired directions is a critical part of analysis, and providing data on current situations can realistically highlight the gap between the two states and thereby offer a motivation to change and improve.

II. THE FACTORS

The factors measured through the framework described above are composed of five major dimensions and nineteen categories within those dimensions. Section 1 below describes and defines each major dimension, while Section 2 deals in the same way with the categories that make up each dimension.

1. MAJOR DIMENSIONS

Coordination

Where the making of high-quality operational decisions in the department is dependent upon information, and possibly other forms of support, from (a) people within the department working with each other, and (b) other departments within the organization.

Coordination includes the following categories:

- Degree to which there is a perceived need;
- Quality of interdepartmental coordination;
- Quality of intradepartmental coordination;
- Degree of information-sharing to other departments;
- Degree of information receipt from other departments;

Management Skills

The ability of the department's manager(s), as seen by members of the department, to effectively carry out responsibilities in the following areas:

a)   Planning for department growth,

b)   Managing department growth,

c)   Development of subordinates,

d)   Solving complex problems, and

e)   Making high-quality decisions affecting or establishing company policy.

Management skills include the following categories:

- Policy decision-making;
- Creative problem-solving;
- Planning;
- Subordinate development.

Organization Structure

The degree to which the pattern and nature of relationships, as represented by the organization's structure, is sufficient to support organizational excellence (includes number of people, amount of supervision, whether a manager has an inappropriate number of people reporting to him or her, etc.).

Organization structure includes the following categories:

- Department structure,
- Company structure.

Goals and Directions

The degree to which the short- and long-term goals, objectives, and plans of the organization and of each department are understood clearly.

Goals and directions include the following categories:

- Department goals,
- Company goals.

Organization Climate

The barometer by which pressures, constraints, attitudes of rewards, and attitudes of others are measured inside the department and the degree to which those factors are affecting performance.

Organization climate includes the following categories:

- Conformity,
- Responsibility,
- Standards,
- Rewards,
- Clarity,
- Team spirit.

2. CATEGORIES

Rather than attempt to offer yet another set of definitions for these categories, it may be clearer if we simply list the questions that make up each category. These questions are included in the Interview survey and/or are part of various questionnaires.

Coordination

Need for coordination

Is there, as an integral part of the job of this department, a need for sharing and receiving information? If so, is that sharing and receiving of information necessary to make high-quality, operational (relating to the operation of the department and/or the organization as a whole) decisions? Why?

Interdepartmental coordination

Is there a need for such information-sharing between this department and other departments? Which ones? To what extent are those, and is this, department(s) dependent upon such information? For which specific decisions? What is the specific flow of information from this department to others? How is it transmitted?

Intradepartmental coordination

Is there a need for such information-sharing among people in this department to make high-quality decisions? Which decisions? Is there a systematic process for determining dimensions of "quality and acceptance" when decisions are to be made? Who is responsible for these decisions?

Information-sharing to others

Do people in this department have the information from others in this department that they need to know to do their jobs effectively (including financial figures, quality reports, job specifications, etc.)? How does this department offer information to others in the organization (i.e., hold regular meetings, distribute memos, or wait for others to come with a question)? Is the information offered to others adequate for them to do an effective job?

Information receipt from others

Do people in this department receive from other departments the information they need to do their jobs effectively? In what form is it presented? Is that information received on a timely basis? If not, is it usually very late or just slightly overdue? How often must you ask for clarification of such information because it is unclear? Rank those departments which offer information, in terms of the adequacy of that information.

Management Skills

Policy decision-making

Is there a need for this department to make decisions that establish or change company policies? If so, in what areas? How (by what specific process) are those decisions made? How much time does the department (as a whole) spend in the decision-making process? How are responsibilities delineated for policy decision-making?

Creative problem-solving

Is there a need for this department to solve problems that are complex in nature? If so, how much time is spent? What specific problem-solving process is used (what steps are taken)? Do people in this department tend to wait for problems to occur or do they anticipate problems by actively and continuously sensing problem symptoms?

Planning

Does this department establish goals and plans for the future on at least an annual basis? Is there a stated demand from the company's top management that planning occurs? What is the process (specific steps taken) for that planning? In general, how specifically are goals and action steps stated? Who within the department is involved in this planning? Who spends the most time? The least time? Who is primarily responsible for managing this planning process?

Development of subordinates

Are performance reviews done on a regular basis? What is the average time span between reviews in the department? Is personal goal-setting done on an individual basis with the department manager? Is personal goal-setting done on a regular basis? Beyond formal reviews, is both positive and negative feedback on performance offered regularly in this department? Are people in this department encouraged to attempt challenging, new undertakings? Are people given sufficient support in this department? By whom? Are outside professional-development programs encouraged in this department? How many people attend at least one each year? Is the department manager easily accessible?

Organization Structure

Department structure

Is there an appropriate number of employees in this department? If not, are there too many or too few in terms of achieving department objectives? Given department goals, is there an appropriate number of supervisors or managers? If not, are there too many or too few? Does information pass easily from one level of the department to another? Does it take too long to hear that a decision has been made by the department manager? Does it take too long to pass information from lower levels in the department to the department manager?

Company structure

Does the organization have a relatively flat or vertical structure? Are there too many/too few/just enough supervisors and managers in the organization? Are there sufficient numbers of hourly workers in the organization to achieve production goals? If not, are there too few or too many? What vehicle is used to pass information from the top of the organization downward (e.g., memos, word of mouth, large meetings, chain of command, none of these, etc.)?

Goals and Directions

Department goals

What are the major objectives of the department for the next year? How were those objectives set (i.e., did the whole department participate in establishing them, or were they established by the department manager)? How many people will belong to this department in five years? Why? What kind of work will this department be doing in five years?

Company goals

What are the major objectives of the company for the next year? How were those objectives set? What business is your company in? What is its major purpose? What will sales volume be in two years? in five years? How are company goals communicated throughout the organization? What is the major obstacle to your company in achieving its goals? Is there too much/not enough/adequate time spent on developing company goals?

Organization Climate

Conformity

What are the feelings of people in this department about the rules and regulations in this company? Are there too many procedures to follow? Does the number of rules and regulations hinder effective performance in this department?

Responsibility

Do people in this department assume responsibility for tasks easily? Typically, does the department manager give directions about what he or she wants done, or do people identify and take on specific tasks on their own?

Standards

Do people in this department constantly try to do an excellent job? Do people in this department tend to want to accomplish tasks quickly so they can move on to something else? Do people in this department tend to do only what is expected of them and, in turn, expect others to do their share? Are hiring criteria in this department too high, too low, or just about right?

Rewards

Are people in this department fairly compensated for the work they do? If not, is the compensation too high or too low? Do people in this department tend to know what others in the department think of them? How (by making assumptions, through continual feedback, etc.)?

Clarity

Are roles and responsibilities clearly defined in this department? Is your department well-organized? If not, why?

Team spirit

Does this department work together as a closely-knit team? Are there decisions made by the whole deaprtment? What are some examples? Is it important to have a warm, friendly relationship among people in this department? Why?

III. DESCRIPTION OF INSTRUMENTS UTILIZED IN OMD DIAGNOSIS

The OMD portion of our diagnosis was carried out through both self-administered instruments and personal interviews with each of the personnel who participated. To offer a clearer understanding of our methodology, a brief description of the instruments used is offered below.

1. THE CLIMATE QUESTIONNAIRE

This instrument is designed to increase the understanding of the type of climate or work environment in which employees find themselves, how this climate is created, and how it affects each person's levels of performance and satisfaction. The questionnaire is divided into two parts; the first asks what the organizational climate actually is in one's department or work unit, and the second asks people to define what they would like it to be.

2. THE WORK-ANALYSIS QUESTIONNAIRE

This questionnaire is designed to discover the demands and pressures placed on an individual by his or her work. It also can determine how those demands and pressures affect performance and satisfaction.

3. THE UNIT ANALYSIS

This instrument seeks information regarding people's attitudes and opinions of several working units. The questions are designed to elicit feelings regarding adequacy of output and of support given by these units.

4. THE OMD MAPPING QUESTIONNAIRE

This questionnaire is designed to probe the feelings and attitudes of people in one's own department and to identify the specific managerial characteristics through which the departmental operations are maintained.

IV. RATINGS, AND FACILITATING AND HINDERING FACTORS PRESENTED BY DEPARTMENT

Presented in this section are the results of our OMD departmental diagnosis. The data is presented in two ways for each department—first, there is one page that summarizes the ratings for the department according to the major dimensions defined above (i.e., coordination, management skills, etc.) and that also lists a rating for the overall management performance of the department. The second part of the data presentation for each department is a series of factors that are termed hindering factors (those factors that could serve as barriers to becoming an excellent organization), and facilitating factors (those factors that could be seen as strengths and could help in achieving excellence). There is also a summary presented for each department, which is intended to highlight some major points or conclusions and certainly is not intended to encompass all of the data gathered for each department.

Sample forms, charts, mappings, and questionnaires based on an actual case history are included, for two important departments. The questionnaires are printed in full as an indication of the thoroughness of the analysis.

PURCHASING

There were major disagreements in the assessment of effectiveness of the purchasing function. Upon probing, it became apparent that there was no clear agreement in price policy among key executives involved. Thus it was not clear when Purchasing should buy at the lowest price, even though it meant longer delivery times, or should buy at higher prices to assure quicker delivery. It is important that policy be clarified and that Purchasing be given clear guidelines on price and delivery policy.

Figures A1.1 and A1.2 represent guides used in analyzing a

department's degree of coordination, and the method of arriving at a composite rating on the first major dimension.

The paragraphs that follow discuss facilitating and hindering factors, and present a brief summary of the findings. Figure A1.3 is a mapping of the department based on efficiency of resources and management skills. The questionnaire prepared for the analysis of the Purchasing Department concludes this section.

Composite Rating of Purchasing Department

	Dimension	Rating
I	Coordination	3.0
II	Management skills	1.9
III	Organization structure	3.9
IV	Goals and directions	2.4
V	Organization climate	2.5
	Department rating (average)	2.8

Facilitating Factors

There is adequate information received from other departments.

People in general have confidence in the ability of those who comprise this department to be able to perform in a beneficial manner.

There were indications of strong working relationships between this department and the production department.

Hindering Factors

There seems to be insufficient time available to perform this function in an excellent manner; the major reason for this may be that with the people in this department also acting as personnel specialists, there is a limited amount of time available for purchasing.

There is a lack of clearly stated, agreed-upon policies to guide the Purchasing Department in carrying out its functions.

There is insufficient attention paid to, and skills demonstrated in planning for, items such as the Purchasing Department of the future.

Summary

Same point as made in referring to the Accounting Department: Purchasing thinks that coordination is adequate in their relationships with other departments, while other departments feel they are not receiving adequate information from Purchasing.

This, of course, reinforces low scores for information-sharing and interdepartmental coordination, and indicates a lack of feedback and openness between groups.

FUNCTION: Purchasing
RESOURCE EFFICIENCY

Question: EFFECTIVENESS OF CONTROL SYSTEM

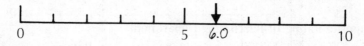

Question: BEST POSSIBLE PRICES

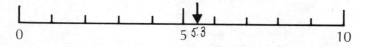

Question: KNOWLEDGE & CONTROL OF VENDORS

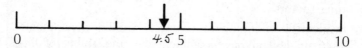

Question: COMMUNICATION WITH MFG & ENGINEERING

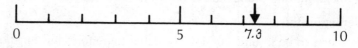

Question:

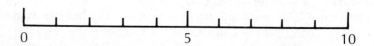

COMPOSITE

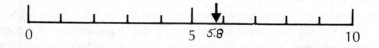

Figure A1.1

Figure A1.2

Subject: **PURCHASING DEPARTMENT**

Questions scored in points as: Poor = 1; Weak = 2; Average = 3; Good = 4; Excellent = 5

No.	QUESTIONS	Product Lines						General
		A	B	C				
1.	How effective is the control system?							3.0
2.	How effective is Purchasing in obtaining best possible prices?							2.9
3.	How adequate is knowledge and control of vendors?							2.3
4.	How good is communication with Engineering and Manufacturing?							3.6
	COMPOSITE						(Average)	2.9

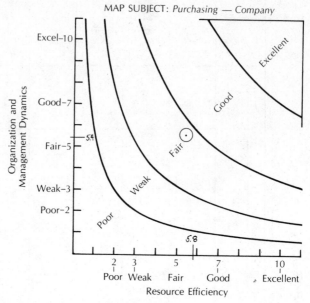

Figure A1.3

Time available to devote to purchasing is at a premium and is a barrier to performing in an excellent manner.

Questionnaire for Purchasing Department

There are four major topics covered herein. Please rate each topic on a 1-to-5 scale based on consideration of the questions included under each topic:

5 = Excellent
4 = Good
3 = Fair, Average
2 = Satisfactory
1 = Poor

1.   *How effective is the control system?*

Is there a requisition for each purchase order?

Is there a purchase order for each purchase?

Is a traveling requisition used for standard items?

Is there a procedure for handling quick minor purchases (less than $10)?

Is there an ability to respond to requests for rush purchases through telephone ordering?

Are telephone orders always tied to a purchase-order number and followed up by necessary paper work?

Is procedure adequate for checking delivery receipts versus purchase orders?

Is procedure adequate for making sure all purchases get into accounts payable?

Is a file kept of delivery receipts being held awaiting receipt of invoices?

How quickly does Purchasing receive copies of delivery receipts?

How many places are records kept of outstanding purchase orders?

Do they all agree?

Are there dollar limits on purchasing by various departments without top executive approval?

Are discounts for prompt payment taken?

Are utility bills audited?

Are scrap sales controlled for weight?

Is there a Purchasing Variance report issued routinely?

2.   *How effective is Purchasing in obtaining best possible prices?*

Are prices obtained from several vendors for each purchase?

Are price breaks taken advantage of?

Does Purchasing consider economic balance between price breaks and inventory costs?

Does Purchasing solicit information on lower prices for larger quantities than vendor reports in price schedules?

Are blanket orders used with release dates furnished as material is required?

Are purchase items classified by ABC?

3.   *How adequate is knowledge and control of vendor?*

Is there a regular procedure for obtaining information on vendors for new items?

Is there an adequate file on vendors used or considered, with vendor capability described?

Is incoming merchandise inspected for quality?

Is poor-quality merchandise returned to vendors?

Is record kept of vendor conformance to quality standards?

Is record kept of vendor conformance to promised delivery dates?

Is vendor notified of ratings on quality and delivery?

How are long-lead purchase items controlled and maintained?

Is control kept on receipts expected, by telephoning vendors as soon as merchandise is late?

4. *How good is communication with Engineering and Manufacturing?*

Do Engineering and Manufacturing provide adequate specifications for Purchasing?

If there is any variation in price or specification from initial purchase specifications or vendor preliminary quotes, is Engineering or Manufacturing contacted?

If there is variation from specifications on delivery, is Engineering or Manufacturing contacted before action is taken?

Can Purchasing respond to emergency situations requiring rapid purchasing actions?

Where Engineering must handle purchase because of technical details, is there a regular procedure for obtaining necessary paper work?

PRODUCTION AND INVENTORY PLANNING & CONTROL

While this function rated weak in many areas, it is not clear from the mapping analysis what opportunities exist for improvements in cost and productivity by adopting more sophisticated techniques in requirements planning, inventory planning and control, and production control. It appears that few opportunities exist with respect to Product A, but it is possible that a significant payoff could be obtained by improvements with respect to Products B and C.

The recent physical inventory variances suggest that item control is not as effective as expected.

Figures A1.4 through A1.9 are guides used in analyzing the department, and are followed by a composite rating. The paragraphs that follow discuss facilitating and hindering factors, and present a brief summary of the findings. Figure A1.10 is a mapping of the department based on efficiency of resources and management skills. The questionnaire prepared for the analysis of this department concludes Appendix 1.

FUNCTION: Inv. & Production Control
RESOURCE EFFICIENCY

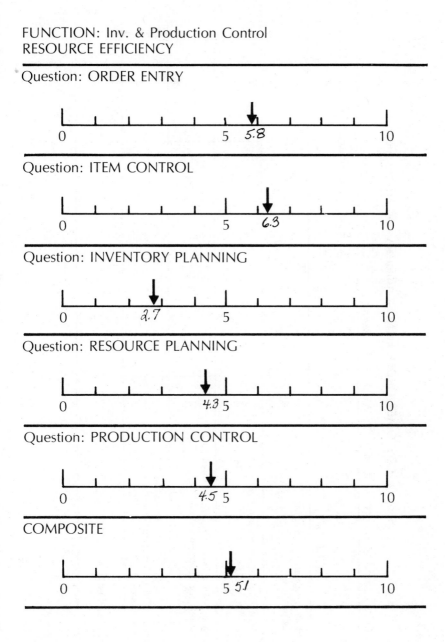

Question: ORDER ENTRY

Question: ITEM CONTROL

Question: INVENTORY PLANNING

Question: RESOURCE PLANNING

Question: PRODUCTION CONTROL

COMPOSITE

Figure A1.4

Figure A1.5

Subject: **CUSTOMER ORDER ENTRY—Adequacy and Effectiveness**

Questions scored in points as: Poor = 1; Weak = 2; Average = 3; Good = 4; Excellent = 5

No.	QUESTION	Product Lines						General
		A	B	C				
1.	How adequate is customer notification?	4	4	5				
2.	How adequate is information on service level?	1	1	1				
3.	How effective is company in meeting targets for customer service?	4	4	3				
4.	How effective is data-processing system in utilizing order-entry information?	4	4	2				
	COMPOSITE	3.2	3.2	2.7				

Figure A1.6

Subject: INVENTORY ITEM CONTROL

Questions scored in points as: Poor = 1; Weak = 2; Average = 3; Good = 4; Excellent = 5

No.	QUESTION	Product Lines A	B	C					General
1.	How adequate is control over issues of finished goods?	4	4	4					
2.	How adequate is control over issues of raw materials? of in-process inventory?	4 5	3 4	5 4					
3.	How adequate is control over replenishment of finished goods?	5	4	3					
4.	How adequate is control over replenishment of raw materials and work in process?	4	4	2					
5.	How effective is perpetual inventory system?	4	3	2					
	COMPOSITE	4.3	3.6	3.3					

Figure A1.7

Subject: **INVENTORY PLANNING**

Questions scored in points as: Poor = 1; Weak = 2; Average = 3; Good = 4; Excellent = 5

No.	QUESTION	Product Lines						General
		A	B	C				
1.	How good is the data base for inventory planning?	2	2	2				
2.	How sophisticated are tools used for planning?	1	1	1				
3.	How comprehensive is inventory planning?	2	2	2				
	COMPOSITE	1.7	1.7	1.7				

Figure A1.8

Subject: **RESOURCE PLANNING**

Questions scored in points as: Poor = 1; Weak = 2; Average = 3; Good = 4; Excellent = 5

No.	QUESTION	Product Lines						General
		A	B	C				
1.	How thoroughly is resource planning done?	2	2	2				
2.	How effective is the planning?	2	2	2				
3.	How adequate is the planning?	2	2	2				
4.	How thorough are the material planning procedures?	3	3	3				
5.	How complete is the data base and information needed for effective planning and scheduling?	4	4	4				
6.	How well does the system provide the capacity to plan; to foresee bottlenecks, shortages, vacuums?	3	3	2				
	COMPOSITE	2.7	2.7	2.5				

Figure A1.9

Subject: **PRODUCTION CONTROL**

Questions scored in points as: Poor = 1; Weak = 2; Average = 3; Good = 4; Excellent = 5

No.	QUESTION	Product Lines							General
		A	B	C					
1.	To what extent is flow through the shop directed according to a defined comprehensive system?	2	2	2					
2.	To what degree does the production control system provide capability to foresee or rapidly spot trouble situations needing corrective action?	2	2	2					
3.	How capable is the system of handling deviant events?	4	4	2					
4.	How adequate is the system?	3	3	2					
	COMPOSITE	2.7	2.7	2.0					

Composite Rating for Production Control and Customer Service Department

	Dimension	Rating
I	Coordination	3.0
II	Management Skills	2.7
III	Organization Structure	3.5
IV	Goals & Directions	1.5
V	Organization Climate	2.4
	Department Rating (average)	2.6

Facilitating Factors

There seem to be good relationships between this department and others it must work together with, as well as adequate and sufficient information flow between departments.

Responsibility has been assumed by this department even when it was not clear how and by whom decisions should be made.

There seems to be a clear desire to assume responsibility and to grow.

Hindering Factors

There is uncertainty in this department regarding specific roles and responsibilities and regarding impressions, reactions, and desires of top management.

The company's long- and short-term goals are unclear, as are goals for the Production Control and Customer Service Department.

Summary

The combination of a high degree of responsibility—to take responsibility for making decisions, seek out ways to improve performance, etc.—and a lack of understanding of roles and responsibilities and lack of feedback from superiors has, understandably, resulted in frustration and confusion within this department.

Major strengths of this department are its willingness to experiment, to take risks, and to improve; such desires must be fostered and encouraged.

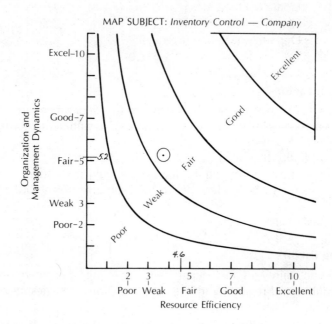

Figure A1.10

Questionnaire for Production & Inventory Planning and Control

1. COST ELEMENTS—INVENTORIES

1. Please fill out the following tabulation concerning inventories and sales. Use the latest period for which figures are available and give date.

Inventory	Product Line						Totals
Raw Matls.—$							
Raw Matls.—Weeks of Stock							
In-Process—$							
In-Process—Weeks of Stock							
Fin. Goods in Plt.—$							
Fin. Goods in Plt.—Weeks of Stock							
Fin. Goods Elsewhere—$							
Fin. Goods Elsewhere—Weeks of Stock							
Total—$							
—Weeks of Stock							
Annual Sales—$							
Ratio— Sales / Inventory							

2. COST ELEMENTS—PLANNING & CONTROL FOR MANPOWER AND EQUIPMENT

1. This tabulation is designed to summarize the labor hours spent per week by those people directly concerned with the planning and controlling of production and inventories. Equipment investment is included also. Note that the EDP operating function is tabulated separately.

	Man-Hours per Week						
	Product Line						
	A	B	C			Gen'l.	Totals
Supervisory							
Clerical—Forecasts							
—Order Entry							
—Inventory Records							
—Material Requirements							
—Production Control							
—Reports							
Equipment $							

3. COST ELEMENTS—FLOOR SPACE

1. Approximately how much floor space (sq. ft.) is occupied by inventories?

Floor Space

	Product Line						Totals
	A	B	C			Gen'l.	
Raw Matls. Storage							
In-Proc. Storage							
Fin. Goods Storage							
Receiving							
Shipping							

Subject: **4. INVENTORY VALUE**

(Enter rating level numbers in table)

No.	QUESTION	Product Lines						
		A	B	C				General
1.	How adequate and accurate is information or value?							
2.	How well is financial value of inventory tied in with perpetual inventory records?							
3.	How significant are inventory write-downs?							

4. INVENTORY VALUE

How are inventories costed?

- Direct Costs
- Total Costs
- Other

Are standard costs used?
What valuation system is used?

- FIFO
- LIFO
- Other

1. *How adequate and accurate is information or value?*

   Frequency of valuing inventories

   > Annually
   > Semi Annually
   > Quarterly
   > Monthly
   > More frequently

   Physical Inventory

   > Annually
   > Semiannually
   > Quarterly
   > Monthly
   > More frequently

   When no physical inventory, how are inventory values determined?

   > Standard Cost System
   > Using Average Gross Margin
   > Based on Volume of Inventory from Perpetual Inventory Records

2. *How well is financial value of inventory tied in with perpetual inventory records?*

   Are costs of each item maintained in an item file?

   Can costs of an item be changed easily for a component item through some type of bill of material processor?

   Do such inventory values agree with financial values at end of accounting period?

   > Within 98%
   > Within 95%
   > Within 90%
   > Less than 90%

3. How significant are inventory write-downs?

Obsolescence write-down: Dollars ____ % of Sales ____

Write-off for change in item valuation: Dollars ____ % of Sales ____

Write-off from returns: Dollars ____ % of Sales ____

Write-down for seconds: Dollars ____ % of Sales ____

Write-off for scrap: Dollars ____ % of Sales ____

Unaccounted for write-offs: Dollars ____ % of Sales ____

Write-off because of difference in count of perpetual and physical inventory: Dollars ____ % of Sales ____

How frequently are write-downs and adjustments made?

Annually
Semiannually
Quarterly
Monthly
More frequently

DESCRIPTION OF SYSTEM

On the next page is a schematic of the major modules inherent in a complete Logistics Control System (materials, men, and machines). The questions which follow are generally structured around these modules.

5. CUSTOMER ORDER ENTRY

A. General

1. What proportion of product is made for special customer orders, and what proportion is made to stock orders?

	Product Line					
	A	B	C			
% Special Order						
% Stock						
	100%	100%	100%	100%	100%	100%

2. Are continuous records kept, by product line and product, of customer orders that form an order history?
(Indicate by check mark if EDP is utilized here).

(Y = Yes; N = No P = Partial)	Product Line					
	A	B	C			
Records Kept?						
—By Product?						
—By Product Line?						
EDP Used?						

3. *Centralization of order entry*

   a) *Orders come to a central place for processing*

   b) *Orders are filled at various locations, with copies to central place*

   c) *Orders scheduled before processing by sales edit*

   d) *Customer order is used for picking*

   e) *Customer orders are reproduced on company forms to produce packing list*

   f) *Post billing procedure with orders picked before inventory records are processed and before invoices are prepared*

   g) *Prebilling procedure with orders processed against inventory records with production of order, back-order, picking list, packing list, bill of lading, and invoices*

B. *Adequacy and Effectiveness*

1. *How adequate is customer notification?*

   Customer advised on receipt of order

   Customer advised of date order expected to be shipped

   Customer advised of back ordered items and expected date of shipment of back orders

   Customer advised of any change in promised shipment

   Customer advised when order shipped

2. *How adequate is information on service level?*

   Records kept of:

   Dollars, no. and % of lines filled

   Dollars, no. and % of items filled

   Dollars, no. and % of orders shipped complete

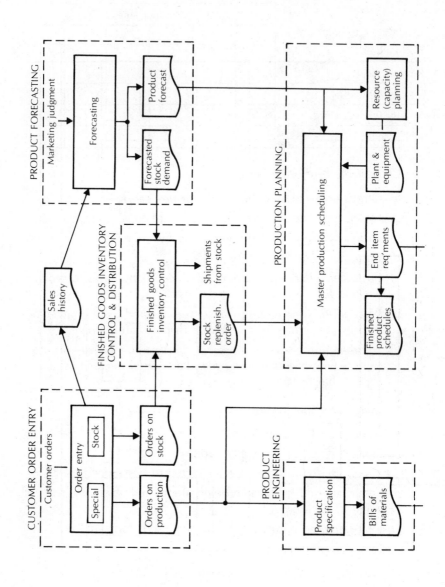

Figure A1.12

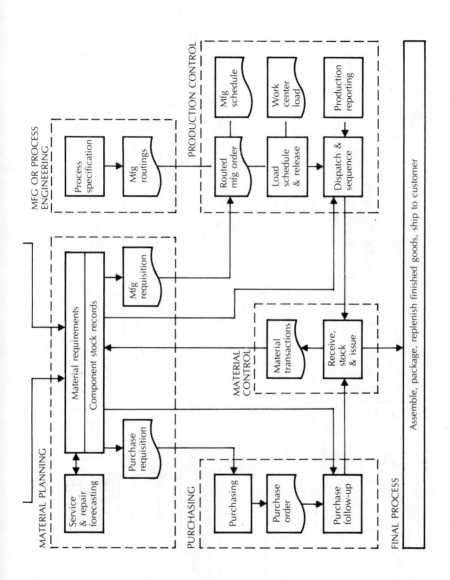

Subject: 5. CUSTOMER ORDER ENTRY

B. Adequacy And Effectivness—Summary Sheet

(Enter rating level numbers in table)

No.	QUESTION	Product Lines						General
		A	B	C				
1.	How adequate is customer notification?							
2.	How adequate is information on service level?							
3.	How effective is company in meeting targets for customer service?							
4.	How effective is data-processing system in utilizing order-entry information?							

Time to pick order

Time to process order

Time from dispatch of order from customer to receipt at order entry

3. *How effective is company in meeting targets for customer service?*

Are targets established in terms of time to process and ship an order?

Are targets established in terms of desired % of lines shipped within a specific time period?

Are targets established in terms of desired % of items shipped within a specific time period?

Are targets established in terms of desired % of orders shipped complete within a specific time period?

How well does company meet targets on weekly, monthly, and annual basis?

Within 2%

Within 5%

Within 10%

4. *How effective is data processing system in utilizing order-entry information?*

Daily reports on number and value of orders

Order data used for forecasting and to track forecast

Order data becomes survey information for sales analysis by customer and product

Information is valuable on current basis for control as well as history.

6. COMPONENT, WORK-IN-PROCESS, AND RAW MATERIAL INVENTORIES

a) How many component and raw material items are controlled?

b) How many are active?

c) How many levels are there from raw materials to finished goods?

d) How many are controlled?

e) What is the average number of levels per bill of material?

f) What is the average and range of the number of components per bill of material?

g) What is the amount of unplanned issues processed?

h) What is the average and range of part lead times (made and bought)?

Subject: 7. INVENTORY ITEM CONTROL

Rate each of these questions on a 1 to 5 scale. (Refer to the detail questions under each on the following pages.)

No.	QUESTION	Product Lines							General
		A	B	C					
1.	How adequate is control over issues of finished goods?								
2.	How adequate is control over issues of raw materials and in process inventory?								
3.	How adequate is control over replenishment of finished goods?								
4.	How adequate is control over replenishment of raw materials and work in process?								
5.	How effective is perpetual inventory system?								

7.   INVENTORY ITEM CONTROL

a)   *How adequate is control over issues of finished goods?*

Is every issue covered by some written document?

Are shipments from finished stock posted against balance on hand before or after picking?

Are shipments checked for count after picking and before shipping?

Does warehouse have a good location system?

If prebilling system used, is the percent of actual out-of-stock vs indication of a balance on hand 10%, 5%, 2%, 1%?

Are all transfers from finished inventory convered by an issue document?

b)   *How adequate is control over issues of raw materials and in-process inventory?*

Are all issues of raw material covered by an issue document or by exploding production?

Are conversions of pounds to units, etc., checked periodically for accuracy?

Are materials issued in bulk to various work centers?

If bulk issues are used, are standards used for issue to products from work centers?

Are variances calculated by work center to which bulk issues are made?

Are counts made at each work center of amounts transferred in?

Are counts made when merchandise is transferred from production to finished inventory?

Are items issued but not used and returned to stock covered by appropriate transfer documents?

Are items returned to stock counted?

Are items issued to outside processors counted and covered by transfer documents?

Is record kept of items at outside processors?

Are items returned by outside processors covered by transfer documents and counted upon receipt?

c)   *How adequate is control over replenishment of finished goods?*

Are all items transferred into finished goods counted?

Are all items transferred into finished goods covered by transfer documents?

Are items returned to finished goods from customers handled in a special department?

Are items counted and checked against authorization for return?

Are returned items inspected and separated into good, reusable items, and those defective in some way?

If so, are defective items subject to counting and regular procedure for write-off and salvage?

Are purchased finished items counted upon delivery, inspected, and transferred to finished inventory with appropriate transfer documents?

d) *How adequate is control over replenishments of raw materials and work-in-process?*

Are incoming goods inspected, counted, and checked against packing lists and bills of lading?

Are incoming goods checked against purchase orders?

Are defective goods returned to vendors?

Are incoming goods transferred to inventory upon receipt of goods or upon receipt of invoices?

Are outlying warehouse records updated for replenishment immediately upon transfer from central warehouse, or is an in-transit inventory maintained?

e) *How effective is perpetual inventory system?*

How well do receiving reports reconcile with purchase orders?

Are stock rooms locked?

Is cycle counting of inventories used?

Are records checked whenever zero balances are reached?

Is there a significant deterioration in accuracy of records as time from last physical inventory increases?

Can balances for all items be determined quickly and easily?

Is there a significant time lag between physical movement in and out of inventory and updating of inventory records?

Are records manual or automated?

If automated, is there a backup manual record which is more reliable?

How accurate are stock records?

97%
95%
90%
80%
70% or less

8.   INVENTORY PLANNING

a)   *How good is the data base for inventory planning?*

Are records kept for each item showing on hand, on order, available inventory after reservations, date ordered, date received, amount ordered, amount shipped, date ordered (by customer), date shipped?

Are records kept of backorders by product and customer?

Do records show weight and cube of item?

Do records show various shipping packs for each item?

Are transportation costs for key shipping points readily available?

Is the data available for transportation costs per period by freight in, freight out, full car or truck, LCL or LTL, and parcel post?

Does item record show cost?

Is data base automated?

Can costs of higher-level items be updated easily if cost of a lower-level item changes, through some type of bill-of-material processor?

Is data available by location in warehouse?

Is record kept of number of zero balances for an item in a period?

Is data available for replenishment time for each item?

b)   *How sophisticated are tools used for planning?*

Are inventory items classified in ABC categories?

Are there different policies for A, B, and C items?

Are any C items bulk-issued with bin control?

Are order quantities determined by an EOQ or similar formula?

If so, is EOQ changed with changes in use, cost, or interest rate?

Is safety stock used and, if so, is there a formula for calculating safety stock based on lead item, EOQ, usage, and service level devised?

Are there allocation rules and procedures?

Is some form of priority or critical-ratio formula used for truck loading for replenishment shipments?

Subject: **8. INVENTORY PLANNING**

Rate each of these questions on a 1 to 5 scale. (Refer to the detail questions under each on the following pages.)

No.	QUESTION	Product Lines						General
		A	B	C				
1.	How good is the data base for inventory planning?							
2.	How sophisticated are tools used for planning?							
3.	How comprehensive is inventory planning?							

Are EOQ quantities rounded to minimum pack quantities?

Is a material requirement planning system used for lower level replenishment?

Is a computer used for inventory planning and control?

Are items classified in terms of fast and slow movement?

Can average usage be readily calculated?

Can standard deviations in usage or forecasts be readily calculated?

c) *How comprehensive is inventory planning?*

Are inventory levels and costs balanced against shipping and production costs?

Is inventory used to balance production levels?

Are there predetermined service levels and do they vary by A, B, and C items?

Do actual service levels correspond closely to predetermined goals?

Is inventory built up to take care of seasonal peaks?

Is inventory available to meet special promotions?

Is there a safeguard in inventory formulas to guard against obsolescence?

If more than one warehouse exists, have inventory levels at each warehouse been balanced against shipping and warehousing costs to determine optimum number of warehouses?

Can inventory levels be simulated to determine impact of policy changes?

9. RESOURCE PLANNING

a) *How thoroughly is resource planning done?*

Is there an estimate of manufacturing requirements for the next six months to a year?

Is the estimate based on specific end products?

Are these end products estimated requirements converted to gross requirements for subassemblies, manufactured parts, and purchased parts?

Are the gross requirements reduced to net requirements based on inventories and various levels and EOQ's?

Are the net requirements time-phased by periods?

Are manpower requirements derived from the estimated net parts requirements?

Subject: 9. RESOURCE PLANNING

Rate each of these questions on a 1 to 5 scale. (Refer to the detail questions under each on the following pages.)

No.	QUESTION	Product Lines			General
		A	B	C	
1.	How thoroughly is resource planning done?				
2.	How effective is the planning?				
3.	How adequate is the planning?				
4.	How thorough are the material planning procedures?				
5.	How complete is the data base and information needed for effective planning and scheduling?				
6.	How well does the system provide the capacity to plan; to foresee bottlenecks, shortages, vacuums?				

Are machine/work center loadings derived from the net parts requirements?

Is a master schedule developed from this net requirements explosion?

Is the master schedule revised regularly? How frequently? Does revision require a total new explosion?

b)   *How thorough is the planning?*

Does long-range planning serve as a constraint on production planning?

Does long-range planning control the procurement of long lead time items or materials?

Does long-range planning have an impact on:

   Sales delivery promises?
   Manning of work centers?
   Acquisition of equipment?
   Inventory financing?
   Venders or subcontractors?

Are inventory levels balanced against production levels to achieve an optimum cost?

Is there close communication between planning, purchasing, and vendors?

c)   *How adequate is the planning?*

What is delivery performance to promise date for nonstock items?

What is productivity performance?

   <u>Standard hours (dollars) produced</u>
        total factory payroll

To what extent is the production load leveled out over the planning period?

Are bottlenecks in equipment and manpower foreseen and alleviated?

d)   *How thorough are the material planning procedures?*

The questions herein generally imply that a computer is used; the same functions however, could be performed manually though it might not be feasible to do so.

   Is a computer utilized in the material planning procedures?

   Are dependent demand items (components, raw materials) controlled by reorder point (ROP) or material requirement planning (MRP)?

If ROP:
    Is there a reservation system?
    How far ahead are items reserved?
    Are requirements consolidated?

If MRP:
    Daily, weekly, or monthly analysis?
    Regeneration or net change?
    Exception report or full report?

Can system work with kits? With option lists? With phantom assembly numbers?

Are family groups recognized?

Are spares and service parts taken into account?

How are orders released to shop:
    controlled to start date or released as ordered?

How are component orders rescheduled:
    by master schedule or independent of end item date?

e) *How complete is the data base and information needed for effective planning and scheduling?*

Are bills of material and routing sheets prepared for orders by the computer?

Is there a defined, disciplined procedure to assure that product changes are reflected in the bills of materials?

Are bills used to generate issue lists and turn-around documents?

Are routing and operation sheets available for all parts?

How accurate are bills of material?

Are change procedures well disciplined?

f) *How well does the system provide the capability to plan; to foresee shortages, bottlenecks, vacuums?*

Are requirements time-phased?

Are lead times incorporated in the system logic? For both shop and vendors?

Does ordering logic allow for setups?

Are work-center capacities measured?

Is manufacturing labor content by work center known for each item? Is this a part of the logic?

What is the time interval of the planning periods? When is the schedule frozen?

Subject: **10. PRODUCTION CONTROL— INFORMATION**

Rate each of these questions on a 1 to 5 scale. (Refer to the detail questions under each on the following pages.)

No. QUESTION	Product Lines				General
	A	B	C		
1. How many orders are in process?					
2. What is the average time in process?					
3. How many work centers?					
4. How many operations per order? (Average and range)					
5. What is the lot size? (Average and range)					
6. What is the run length?					
7. What is the average queue size ahead of a work center?					
8. How much work-in-process in terms of dollars?					
9. How much in terms of days?					

Subject: **10. PRODUCTION CONTROL**

Rate each of these questions on a 1 to 5 scale. (Refer to the detail questions under each on the following pages.)

No.	QUESTION	Product Lines			General
		A	B	C	
1.	To what extent is flow through the shop directed according to a defined comprehensive system?				
2.	To what degree does the production control system provide capability to foresee or rapidly spot trouble situations needing corrective action?				
3.	How capable is the system of handling deviant events?				
4.	How adequate is the system?				

On specials, is the engineering work load and schedule recognized in the planning?

How valid are due dates?

Are past-due items rescheduled?

Is performance to plan measured?

10. PRODUCTION CONTROL

a) *To what extent is flow through the shop directed according to a defined comprehensive system?*

Are orders marked with due dates which are realistic in terms of the production plan?

Are orders released to the shop in accordance with the plan?

Are decisions with respect to 2nd and 3rd shifts, overtime, and new equipment needed, based on a master schedule?

Is the plant workload smoothed out through master scheduling?

Is the number of people required at each work center controlled by master schedule?

Are customer orders and inventory replenishment orders handled on a due-date basis?

Who is responsible for schedule conformance: foreman? dispatcher? production control?

Is there an expediting plan based on critical ratio or the equivalent?

Are there tooling schedules?

b) *To what degree does the production control system provide capability to foresee or rapidly spot trouble situations needing corrective action?*

Is information available as to the location of each order released to the plant?

Are daily reports produced showing jobs at each work center?

Are these jobs summarized in terms of hours required at this work center to complete them?

Are input and output rates measured by work center?

Are queues measured?

Is schedule performance measured?

Is machine utilization measured?

Is production reporting:
automated? by operation or at end of shift? to central source or at work station?

c)   *How capable is the system of handling deviant events?*

Are alternative routings used? Are they retained?

Are there defined procedures for handling job splits, scrap, rework?

Is rework kept separate from virgin production?

Is there a defined system for processing engineering changes to work in process?

Is there a defined system for handling overrides to priorities?

Is the foreman given latitude in scheduling job sequence?

d)   *How adequate is the system?*

How closely are due dates met by work centers? 95%; 90%; 85%; 70%; less?

How many shortages occur due to manufactured parts?

How many orders are started late? Percentage?

How many orders are completed late? Percentage? Give average and range.

How many expediters are there?

Are queues larger than needed to cover variation in input?

Are piece counts accurate at work centers?

How frequently are production runs interrupted due to emergency priorities?

Are long-running jobs overlapped?

Case Study: MRP at Nordberg Machinery Group
(A Division of Rexnord)

INTRODUCTION *

This is a story of bringing a large, complex, job shop under detailed planning and control of its *daily production activities*. Such a feat was almost impossible prior to the 1970's and few (probably less than 5%) have achieved it since then. This is in spite of the APICS (American Production & Inventory Control Society) MRP Crusade of 1972–74 because most of these systems were of the "requirements regenerations type" that connected shop orders to customer and Master Schedule stock orders only once a month or biweekly at best. Nordberg's MRP is a "daily net change" system that responds each day to new repair part orders and scrap replacements, and changes in master schedule requirements.

In order to evaluate the significance of daily net change, it would be helpful to explain why it is so beneficial to large job shops.

First, most expediting systems work on shortages or priorities needed today or each week; obviously a system that responds monthly or biweekly will not be able to replace this manual function.

Second, close-in priorities facilitate the achievement of a low work-in-process inventory; systems that are 2 to 4 weeks out of alignment normally require more inventory and shop space.

Third, if only 5–10% of the records are active each day, why not have a system that reacts to these changes only, which is more efficient than one that re-explodes.

Fourth, provides the ability to prioritize the "past due."

Nordberg's actual results reflect these benefits and are achieving real dollar savings and reductions in Inventory levels.

BACKGROUND

In the late 1960's and early 1970's, the Nordberg Manufacturing Company (later a part of Rexnord) was experiencing severe competitive pressures in the areas of product lead times. This competition strained the resources which were required to conduct the business such as people, materials, equipment, and capital.

Management implemented a computerized job-shop manufacturing control to reduce lead times and save inventories by a more effective

---

*Case Study prepared by Robert Schoner, President, Process Machinery Division, Nordberg Machinery Group, Rexnord Corporation; Engene Schloesser, Manager, EDP Systems, Nordberg Machinery Group, Rexnord Corporation; and Arnold Putnam, President, Rath & Strong, Inc.

utilization of operators, machines, and assembly areas. In addition to the development of the system, basic reliable operating data such as manufacturing-oriented bills of material, manufacturing routings, inventory and shop load reports also had to be developed or extracted from manual records and loaded into the computer.

By 1973, a conversational-mode material-requirements planning inventory system, with manual interrupt between stock levels, was developed and made operational. Orders were scheduled manually and entered into the shop load. A shop-floor control system was developed and implemented with daily dispatch lists generated from the computer. Shop packets were generated from the computer. Labor was reported through a data collection system to a central dispatch operation. A computerized standard data system was also implemented to calculate operations feeds and standard hours, which were used to schedule items and evaluate actual labor performance. Shop labor performance reports were issued daily. The overall shop input was controlled by a Master Scheduling system.

While technology available in the past justified the previous approach, continued independent data-base operations were no longer justified. Technology in the data base and high-capacity disk drive area had already reached that stage that makes a central data-base system feasible.

Therefore, in 1972, a commercially available data-base maintenance system (TOTAL) was purchased. This system was to be used to develop a centralized data base in which all operating data would be stored and maintained for use by all application systems, thereby eliminating the administrative, timing, cost, and accuracy problems of a multiple data-base system.

In late 1973, most systems were operating on the data base system and further corporate business growth projections indicated that there would be need to implement programs to further improve return on assets.

The effect of these efforts through 1974 was to increase inventory turnover from 1.6 for the years 1967 through 1970 to 2.10 in 1974 on a representative major product line. This was made possible by Master Scheduling and substantial manual support of the gross MRP system. The capital investment in inventory which was avoided due to higher turnovers was $3,700,000 in 1974. Plant output was increased significantly due to more effective use of operators, machines, and floor space. Manufacturing became more consistent in meeting schedules and commitments, and reduced product lead times contributed to an increase in business booked.

NEED FOR "DAILY NET CHANGE" MRP

While results to date were impressive, there were significant problems which remained. One of the most important of these was the time required to reflect a change in Master Schedule or upper-level requirements to all lower levels of the product structure. As previously mentioned, a conversational Material Requirements Planning (MRP) system* was operational but required 3 to 4 weeks to replan requirements through all levels to reflect changes in Master Schedules. While this was a considerable improvement over the old manual system (which was almost impossible to replan) it was still not responsive enough to the business activity which occurred during a three- to four-week period. Too much lead time was lost on low-level items due to the length of the replanning cycle.

A second problem was a possible loss in requirements continuity and integrity due to manual intervention through all levels of the product structure from both the *quantity* and *date required* point of view. Lower level dependent demand requirement quantities and due dates frequently were out of phase with the upper level requirements. As a result, there was no positive assurance that lower level planning was in phase with the Master Schedules or upper level requirements.

A third problem, which was related to the second, was the human error factor. Although reduced considerably from the manual system, errors still occurred often enough to affect the accuracy of the system, resulting in higher inventories or shortages and losses in income due to shipments which were delayed by shortages.

MRP SYSTEM FEATURES

At the Nordberg Machinery Group, all programs which would contribute to a reduction in inventories were reviewed. One of those programs reviewed was the accelerated installation of a fully mechanized net change Requirements Planning system. While a substantial reduction in inventory had been achieved through earlier systems installations, it was clear that more could be achieved with the installation of a net-change MRP system. In view of the immediate need and the delays experienced with the development program, three alternatives to advance the installation of a net-change, fully mechanized MRP system were examined: Design and install the system using entirely in-house resources; subcontract the development of a system; or purchase an existing system and modify it as

---

*This system required manual replenishment order planning by inventory analysts at each level in the bill of material.

required. The first alternative was ruled out due to the time required, the lack of in-house development personnel, and the application of existing systems personnel to current systems support. The second was ruled out also due to the lack of time and to the efforts which would be required by systems and user personnel to acquaint a development house personnel with the business and its requirements.

The third was considered the most desirable approach particularly when it was recognized that a net change MRP system was available which included most of the features required by the Nordberg Machinery Group. These key features were:

1. Net Change

A method of adjusting planning by exception rather than total re-explosion of requirements. Repair parts orders are entered daily and their impact on orders, due dates, etc., reflected the following morning.

2. Detail (Pegged) Requirements

A technique of all pertinent audit trails and data integrity. If one or more product assemblies are advanced or retarded in the production schedule, or repair shipments are greater or less than expected, the impact on dates required are reflected in Manufacturing and Purchasing on the following morning.

3. Priorities

A concept that prioritizes production schedules to the true needs. Past due and future dates are appropriately treated.

4. Requirement and Replenishment Modularity

A method which recognizes the possibility of a difference between the need and the present procurement plan for any item.

5. Daily Replanning

A technique to recognize the previous plan. Since this method explodes to all levels, it is more efficient than most expediters and schedule adjusters.

6. Replanning

The replanning can be carried through to the Shop-Floor Control System in updated queue lists and workloads.

7. Separate Recording of Different Kinds of Demand

The usage for production and the usage for service of the same item and the issue to each is differentiated in the system.

8.   Use Allocation Logic

A method to recognize the status of both requirements and replenishments as being planned, signaled, released, picked, or short.

9.   Direct Feedthrough of "Need Date" Adjustment

Using direct feed-through of "need date" adjustment to released shop orders on file as well as to planned orders. Use different algorithms for manufacturing and purchasing action.

Other Advantages

In addition to the foregoing, there were other advantages of the system which involved the environmental aspects of an installation of a net change MRP system. These advantages were:

1. Used proven implementation programs covering complex steps of moving from simple regeneration to optimum net-change capabilities and from gross explosions to netting explosions.

2. Participation by a group that has installed the system elsewhere, with enough internal involvement to assume maintenance responsibility.

3. The system chained together heavily interactive files and those for on-line work.

4. Cost-effective netting and exploding for Material Requirements Planning, resulting in reduced computer run time requirements.

MRP SYSTEM IMPROVEMENT

The system purchased was the Rath & Strong net change MRP system called PIOS.* While the PIOS system included most of the features required by the Nordberg Machinery Group, modifications were required to interface with the existing in-house-developed operating systems and to provide additional features which would allow it to be used in a major job-shop environment. Some of these features were:

1. Ability to retain the structural image of a contract as it was planned from the bill of material and modified through successive engineering changes, to replan the contract in its modified form, and to generate or regenerate contract assembly specifications reflecting all engineering changes.

2. Ability to release individual contract items for planning and ordering action through MRP on an "as designed" basis without having completed Bill of Material structures.

---

*PIOS (Production and Inventory Optimization System) was developed in conjunction with and is jointly owned by Rath & Strong and the Jones and Lamson division of Waterbury Farrel (A Textron Company). The revised version on the TOTAL DATA BASE is jointly owned with Nordberg.

3. Firm planned orders to be used to manually level load work centers. This feature avoided work center overload that might be created by the normal MRP explosion.

The first type of Firm Planned Order is the completely firm order described in current P & IC literature. The order remains fixed in time and quantity until released by Production Control.

The second FPO we call a "hybrid." It remains fixed in time and quantity until a requirement appears that indicates an earlier date is necessary. The order is scheduled inward, never outward. This allows Production Control to plan using the FPO concept, yet retain the flexibility of responding to actual requirements as they appear.

A management report shows the impact of implementing FPO dollars by period of excess inventory and/or potential shortages.

4. Conversion of the PIOS MRP Modules to the TOTAL data-base system.

5. Creation of proper interfaces with other systems within the data base.

6. Inclusion of implosion or where used logic to determine the effects on contract shipping dates of changes in availability of lower level components due to scrap, losses, or missed vendor deliveries.

7. Modification of PIOS output to provide additional information and to produce the information in a format similar to the format of output of the replaced conversational system for order and inventory status inquiry.

8. Expanded Order Logic Operations

    (a) Discrete

    This provides one for one correspondence between requirements and replenishments, especially appropriate for nonstock items.

    In addition, a user-specified portion of the order number is carried down through the explosion in order to provide project order control and accountability.

    (b) Periods of Supply

    For those who wish a closer control over inventory turnover than is provided by standard EOQ logic, this option has been added.

9. Completely Flexible Planning Horizon

    The user can specify as many weekly buckets as desired—both past due and future. This flexibility can be invaluable when critical raw materials develop unusually long lead times.

10. Order Master File and Linkage to Requirements and Replenishments

    This new capability permits explosion downward to analyze the status of a customer order, as well as implosion upward to determine which customer orders may be affected by scrap, late deliveries, etc.

These features added to the PIOS MRP system resulted in an extremely powerful inventory planning tool for a job shop operation.

MRP INSTALLATION

The system was installed in December, 1974. There have been virtually no problems encountered in the installation and its operation since installation. This can be attributed to:

a) The data used by the system such as bills of material and inventory records had been in use for some time, allowing data problems to be identified and corrected before installation of MRP.

b) Functional personnel had been oriented to a mechanized inventory conversational planning system and were accustomed to output similar to MRP output.

c) Functional supervisors were intimately involved in the systems modifications.

d) Extensive training sessions were conducted by functional supervisors with functional personnel.

e) Involvement of key in-house systems personnel who participated in the modifications, provided guidance in the data-base and systems interface areas and also now provide post installation systems support.

f) Direct involvement of Rath & Strong personnel in the modification program, including the technical application, project management, and user education levels.

g) Starting with a logical and technically sound MRP net change system.

While these items cover the key points of making an effective MRP installation, enough cannot be said of the user-system-consultant environment. The following problem areas require substantial attention and compromise.

- Satisfy users, yet hold off disruptive changes once the plan is approved.

- Get the programs running and connect them into a complex system.

- Connect the new complex system (an application package or an in-house development) to all of the other operating systems without disrupting current service by handling thousands of details properly.

- Stop the old system and rely on a new one. This is always traumatic—but at Nordberg there was no practical way of parallel running so the user training and involvement had to be clearly established.

Through the nine months of installation period, people lost their tempers, accusations were made and worked out, schedules were delayed and yet the job was successfully carried out and the final conversion went smoothly—a conversion that takes many similar companies two or three times as long with two or three times the cost. Considerable credit in overcoming these difficulties should be given to the Task Force that met weekly to review the program and

- break bottlenecks
- make systems decisions
- establish priorities
- reassign personnel
- revise schedules

In addition to the weekly meetings, many of the Task Force were working together on a daily basis. These included from Nordberg, Frank Strang, Plant Manager, Frank Monfre, Inventory Control Manager, Ron Borowski, Systems Manager, and from Rath & Strong, Woodrow Chamberlain, Senior Consultant and Robert Cronan, Applications Software Consultant.

Major reviews were held monthly by an informed Steering Committee (Nordberg—Robert Schoner, Vice President Operations, Gene Schloesser, EDP Systems Manager; and Rath & Strong—Arnold Putnam, Client Project Officer). The Steering Committee handled major decisions and controversies that could not be settled within the Task Force.

PROVEN RESULTS WITH MRP

With the installation of the net-change MRP system module, the performance of the manufacturing control system improved considerably. The system now has the means of recognizing and responding immediately and accurately to changing conditions which require reaction and planning adjustments, such as an increase or decrease in customer requirements, unplanned independent demands for spares, vendor lead-time changes, shortages, losses due to scrap, and delays in delivery. In addition, it provides the means of identifying short- and long-range requirements for capacity planning or long-term vendor capacity negotiations. In so doing, it reduces the day-to-day crisis operations of the past which were brought about by the inability to plan future requirements.

The overall effect is planning which creates a more stable, efficient, productive, lower-cost, manufacturing orientation operation.

It is expected that the effect of the installation of a net-change MRP system will not be fully reflected until 1976 when inventory turnovers of a major product line will increase to 2.35 from the 2.10 previously achieved. The avoided capital investment due to this increase in turnover is expected to be in the area of $2,800,000 or a total of $5,600,000 for one product line. Increases in the turnover are also projected in 1977 and 1978, resulting in an even greater avoided capital investment. Shipments exceed forecast for 16 out of 17 months. In spite of lower inventory, customer service on repair-parts orders improved substantially. (Historically, shipments of new machines did not reach targets 50% of the time and customers complained about slow repair-part service.)

A recent analysis of one particular product line (valves) revealed some astounding results. Comparing Pre-MRP 1974 with Post-MRP 1975:

- Billings were up 50%.

- Bookings were down 40%.

- While finished inventories were up (to support the higher billing rate), work-in-process and raw materials were down (in response to the lower booking rate).

- Overall inventories were down 13%.

- On-time deliveries averaged 90–95% during 1975.

- Inventory turnover increased from 1.1 to 1.8 times.

In more traditional (EOQ) systems inventory responds to billings. In such systems a 50% increase in billings would produce a 22% *increase* in inventory. Clearly the new MRP system is responding faster and more accurately to changing business conditions than under the old system. It is hard to argue against lower inventories *and* better service.

The Production Control organization, which had been reduced in 1973–74 during an increase in volume, was further reduced with the Daily Net Change MRP system. The total staff reduction is now 10 or about 15%.

The products are capital goods with low volumes, high piece-part costs, which had traditionally low inventory turnovers. In view of the anticipated shortage of capital, these products tend to become less and less profitable. However, with the implementation of modern management systems and tools such as net change MRP, not only can they survive, but, in fact, they are increasing their profit contribution and return on capital employed. Nordberg has seen a change in return on assets from about 3% in 1970 to 13% in 1974 and to about 25% in 1975.

Software Packages for Manufacturing Applications

INTRODUCTION *

It is impossible to be complete and difficult to be objective in dealing with this subject. In some areas I am biased because Rath & Strong offers application packages to supplement our consulting services. We also have supplied consulting support on evaluating and installing other Vendors packages. Our obligation in either case is to the client user—not to the Vendor. The intimate knowledge that comes with hands-on experience naturally leads to more detailed criticism than casual acquaintance might generate. Thus, while I may make verbal comments in my talk about some of the suppliers, these are for amplification of a point and not covered in the written text. If you are interested in a specific area, you should investigate (at least in the preliminary stages) all of those application packages that are available. The price ranges shown are approximate, and potential buyers should be aware that the highest price still might be the best bargain. Many application programs are also for rent—the relationship is annual rental $\times$ $4-6$ = Purchase Price. Thus, a $200 per month charge would be equivalent to a $2,400 $\times$ 5 = $12,000 purchase price.

The treatment now proceeds from the beginning—Forecasting and Master Scheduling—to the end—Shop Floor Control and Shipments. It can be argued that Forecasting and Master Scheduling are in the province of General Management or Marketing, but even accepting that, the tie-in to Manufacturing is so important that these areas are included in this Appendix.

OUTLINE

Area of Need	Overview	Approximate Price and Comments
RESOURCE PLANNING (Uses Typical or Representative Models and time phased work requirements—not individual routings)	These packages take a Master Schedule of high level requirements (Model, Quantity, Time Phased) and explodes into Work Center, Time Phased Resource and Manpower Requirements.	Most beneficial to those who do not have full B/M, Routings, and Work Standards available for a complete time-phased explosion of work center loads. Also beneficial to those who have the complete data up, but whose parameters are so wide that it takes 3 or more days for each try at annual requirements. *(Price $5–10K)* There is also an interactive system on a National Time Sharing service.

*Taken from a paper presented to the National AIIE Systems Seminar in Boston, Dec. 1976

Area of Need	Overview	Approximate Price & Comments
CAPACITY PLANNING FINITE (May use all actual Product Structures Routings and alternates)	These programs take high level Master Schedule and explode into Resource and Manpower demands where the resources have limits and the overloads are tested for advance fill or alternate operations and then the balance is forward scheduled into the future.	These have their best application in Process Industries where almost all of the Resources are Fixed Capacity. Most Job Shops, however, prefer to know about overloaded facilities so they can use alternatives of subcontract, overtime, alternate routing, etc., and still meet the desired schedule. (Forward scheduling causes *a failure* to make plan.) In addition, the logic in some of these programs is so complex that jobs disappear from Work Center Queue lists. *(Price $12–25K)*
CAPACITY PLANNING INFINITE (May use actual Structures & Routings	Similar to the Resource Planning except done in more complete detail, may simulate order action individual lead time effect.	Best for those companies with a small or moderate data parameter (i.e. under 15,000 parts × 50 pns = 75,000) *(Price $7–25K)*
FORECASTING	These packages operate on usage and/or demand, usually have 2 or more exponential smoothing options, seasonal weighting, standard or average deviation of actual to forecast. Some may have EOQ simulation capability.	Good for most applications if used properly and not below levels where demand becomes dependent on higher levels of assembly structure. May be valuable for spares and repair parts even where the new products are highly structured and dependent demand related. *(Price $4–15K)*
MRP GROSS REQUIREMENTS REGENERATION	These programs use the Product Structure and Inventory Files. They explode a high level schedule into	This program can only be updated by complete regeneration. For moderate to large data parameters

Area of Need	Overview	Approximate Price & Comments
	all level requirements. Netting against inventory may be done but the on-hand, on-order, or new order quantities are not pegged to the higher level requirement.	regeneration is likely to be monthly, or, at best, every 2 weeks. This usually means that shop due date control will need daily and weekly expediting. *(Price $9–20K)*
DAILY NET CHANGE PEGGED REQUIREMENTS	These programs explode the Master Schedule and create Requirements at all levels, they net against on-hand and on-order and peg all replenishments to all requirements. Because of this, additions and changes can be made daily only to those records affected. Shop dates can be revised daily and new manufacturing and purchase orders generated.	Some of these systems provide a direct link daily to the Production Control system, others don't. This is a key to eliminating expediting personnel. *(Price $20–80K)*
MRP—WITH FIRM PLANNED ORDER FEATURE	The Firm Planned Order locks in manufacturing orders as designated so they cannot be rephased by MRP—this is important where a work center is fully loaded and the schedule should be frozen. A report of the overlaod to MRP is furnished.	This feature is important and only available in a few of the packages. It is the answer to the advocates of Finite Capacity planning that such situations do occur in job shops from time to time and on certain facilities. *(Price Included)*
INVENTORY MODULES	There are some distribution and/or companies with no assembly (basic metals, one piece components) that can operate satisfactorily with a basic Inventory System; these handle Receipts, Invoices, On Order, Reservation, etc., and provide usage history, order quantities, and safety stocks.	These systems can be combined with the Forecasting Modules previously described and work well for the type of company described. *(Price $3–15K)*

Area of Need	Overview	Approximate Price & Comments
SHOP FLOOR SCHEDULING & CONTROL	These systems usually have Input/Output, Work Center Queue Loads with Priority Scheduling Rules. They operate best when connected with a date change adjusted by a daily net change MRP system which responds to scrap, special orders, schedule changes, etc.	There are fewer of these packages available but they are an important part of the job. They are generally less expensive than the MRP modules. *(Price $6–20K)*
SHOP FLOOR CONTROL ONLY	These new systems are of the CRT type rather than the order data collection terminals and operate with improved edit checks, less paperwork and improved on-line statements on order location.	In my opinion, the badge, card reader only data collection type devices will be replaced at an increasing rate by these CRT systems. (Price—May be part of Hardware Suppliers Package—$4–10K)
OPERATION SHEET DEVELOPMENT & MAINTENANCE FOR I.E.'S	These programs develop and maintain Work Measurement standards based upon programs supplied in the application packages. Some of the packages come with time data for Machine Shops, Metal Working, and Assembly operation. Other programs are data independent and use the client's data provided it is properly coded when loaded into storage.	These packages are most valuable to Job Shops, somewhat less for electronic and sheet metal, and of little need to most Process Industries. If the typical company has piece parts with an average of 6 operations each, the data storage involved could be 6 times that needed for Part Master or Routing Master Files. *(Price $6–$15K—Without Time Data)*

RESOURCES

Probably the most complete listing from an EDP viewpoint of all application packages is supplied by Data PRO. Even here, many are not as yet listed. They tend to repeat what has been offered to them without much user evaluation—but from an EDP viewpoint this may be a good start.

The only written evaluation (that I know of) from a user's viewpoint has been made on MRP Programs by Ollie Wight. There is a charge for the analysis and not all MRP systems are covered.

Consequently, these sources as well as my talk can be a starting point, but, potential buyers should look more broadly—but, more importantly, visit the users of the final application programs that they have under consideration.

EVALUATION

The basic economics of application packages is that the initial price should be almost 1/5 to 1/4 of the complete cost to develop a specific system in-house. The difference is not all savings because the buyer has some customizing and some connecting of the system into his other EDP systems. The more complex and the more "mainstream" the programs are, the higher those extra costs become. I will give a couple of extremes to put parameters on the problem:

Application Area	Package Cost	Customizing	Tying Existing Pkg.	Total Pkg. Inst.	In-House Development
Basic Inventory	$10–$15,000	$2–$5,000	$ 5,000	$ 25,000	$ 75,000
MRP	$50,000	$40,000	$40,000	$130,000	$250,000

The simple programs offer greater percentage savings with less adjustment. This has definitely been true of accounting programs of Payroll, Payables, Receivables, and General Ledger.

However, (ignoring percentages) the greatest dollar and time savings will come from the more complex areas like MRP.

In evaluating, one should also consider if the package is available for *their* computer and working under their operating systems and data base Management systems. Most of those currently available are for IBM 360-370 hardware running under DOS. Some are available for other hardware manufacturers and some are available under DL-1 and OS and TOTAL but not as many.

SUMMARY

We believe that Application Programs properly selected and applied will save the user both time and money. We believe that the percentage of application packages used will increase as compared to complete in-house development between now and the early 1980's. The major area of risk and concern has already arisen—

Many reasonably good MRP programs have been sold and are running on *sample data,* but not doing anything for the customer and the users. The purchaser is unhappy because he didn't understand the full magnitude of—

- Customizing costs

- Tie-in to other systems costs

- User training costs

- Data clean up costs

The package vendor may not emphasize the magnitude of these problems since this is the buyer's problem. However, disappointed customers and unused application packages hurt us all—both potential buyers who will be unduly "scared off" and the "tell it like it is" sellers who would have adequately warned the uneducated buyer of the "customizing and connecting up" cost—so be it! In five years we will all know how this comes out.

Index

Index